The 'Benefit' Blueprint for Startup Success

SAMEER BABBAR

SVB

THE 'BENEFIT' BLUEPRINT FOR STARTUP SUCCESS

www.ingramcontent.com/pod-product-compliance
Lightning Source LLC
Chambersburg PA
CBHW071335210326
41597CB00015B/1460

CONTENTS

NATIONAL LIBRARY OF AUSTRALIA CATALOGUING-IN-PUBLICATION DATA

Title: The 'Benefit' Blueprint for Startup Success

Author: Sameer Babbar

ISBN:

- 978-0-9876408-2-6(Paperback)
- 978-0-9876408-3-3(Hardcover)
- 978-0-9876408-4-0(eBook)

Subjects:

- Startups
- Entrepreneurship
- Business strategy
- Customer benefits
- Business development

Dewey Decimal Classification:658.11

Publisher: SVB Group

Publication Date: August 21, 2024

DEDICATION

This book is dedicated to the courageous entrepreneurs who embrace failure as a necessary steppingstone on the path to success. Your unrelenting drive to pursue your dreams, even in the face of setbacks and obstacles, has inspired us all to keep pushing forward. Your innovation and risk-taking have not only helped to create a better world for us, but for future generations as well. Thank you for your unwavering dedication and perseverance.

ACKNOWLEDGEMENT

I am deeply indebted to my friends who have helped me give the right polish to the book - Satvik Sharma who I met while he was studying leadership and management at SP Jain Institute of management, Mahammod Tilly, who is also a co-investor and mentor at Startmate, Brendon Woods a friend and a fellow Rotarian.

I am especially grateful to my lovely family, who have been my supporters along my journey and helped me turn my ideas in this book.

DISCLAIMER

The information contained in this book is for general informational purposes only. The author, their associates, directors, and any other parties affiliated with the production of this book do not guarantee the accuracy, completeness, or usefulness of the information contained herein. The author and affiliated parties specifically disclaim any and all liability for any losses or damages that may result from the use or reliance on this information.

The reader is strongly advised to consult with a legal or financial advisor or consultant before making any decisions or taking any actions based on the information contained in this book. The reader assumes full responsibility for any actions taken based on the information contained in this book, and the author and affiliated parties will not be held responsible for any losses or damages that may result.

By reading this book, the reader agrees to the terms of this disclaimer and releases the author and affiliated parties from any and all liability.

This disclaimer is intended to be as comprehensive as possible, and it is the reader's responsibility to understand and agree to the terms set forth herein. If any part of this disclaimer is found to be unenforceable or invalid, the remaining provisions shall remain in full force and effect.

HOW TO NAVIGATE THIS BOOK

Welcome! This book is crafted as a blueprint, focusing on a pivotal aspect often overlooked: the power of selling benefits over features. In the startups technology reigns, it's crucial to remember that features, while pivotal, are the backstage. It's the benefits that take centre stage, resonating with consumers and investors alike.

As a founder, your time is precious, and your path unique. This book is written with startup founder's agile companion. Founders are hard-pressed for time. I have attempted it be simplistic and super concise and steered clear of. long winded narratives. Dive into sections that resonate with your immediate needs, apply the insights, and see the impact in real-time. Each topic and its examples, is an invitation to transform knowledge into tangible outcomes. Let this book be supplementing your journey.

I trust you'll uncover valuable insights. As you grow, revisit the ideas. You may revisit, relearn, and re implement as your journey evolves. Think of this book as your strategic ally in the startup world. Be patient, be curious, and most importantly, be ready to break the mould and redefine success on your terms.

There is an ongoing challenge of falling in love with our own ideas. Great business comes with falling in love with solving customer problems. Let that be your pursuit.

That said, I'm an email away: to discuss your challenges, and celebrate your milestones. Let's embark on this journey together.

Best wishes,

Sameer Babbar

August 21, 2024

sbabbar@sameerbabbar.com

| 1 |

Introduction

Entrepreneurship and Startups

Let's dive into the world of entrepreneurship, focusing primarily on startups but also touching upon its manifestation as how it transpires into and inspires the corporate environment. While these two paths share a spirit of innovation and risk-taking, they diverge significantly in their nature and challenges.

In the startup world, entrepreneurship is a journey for the bold and visionary. It's about stepping away from the traditional 9-5 routine and embracing a path that often turns into a 24/7 commitment. Here, we're talking about building something from the ground up, often with limited resources and in the face of great uncertainty. It's the pursuit of that elusive 'overnight success' which can take years to achieve in this game. A typical startup founder takes the fall for the rest of us.

The failure rate among startups is extremely high. A fraction of startups will succeed and of the limited fraction, only few successful ones will see past their first decade. The ones that make it, make the pursuit worthwhile. Often the founders of failed startups persist till they succeed. Startups fail, but founders always succeed whether they earn, or they learn.

On the other hand, corporate entrepreneurship, or intrapreneurship, involves innovating within an existing corporate structure. It's about driving change and fostering innovation from within an established organisation. While it offers the stability and resources of a larger company, it also comes with its own set of challenges, like navigating corporate bureaucracy and aligning new ideas with the company's strategic goals. In startups, breaking the mould is often celebrated, while in corporate settings, there's a delicate balance between innovation and conforming to established structures that needs to prevail. Governance and breaking the mould are hard to get along with.

Both paths of entrepreneurship and intrapreneurship require a fusion of innovation and a readiness to embrace risk. As entrepreneurs and intrapreneurs, we are the vanguards who dare to explore uncharted territories, whether it's launching new products, services, or business models in a startup, or driving transformative initiatives in a corporate setting. This endeavour demands creativity, foresight and a profound tolerance for risk...to take the fall. The questions that you should ask yourself now are: is this for me? Am I ready?

Now, let's clear up a common misconception: entrepreneurship, whether in a startup or a corporate environment, is not a haven for the idle seeking shortcuts. Far from it. True entrepreneurship is far from a path of least resistance. It requires relentless dedication, resilience, hard work, and numerous pivots. In both arenas, success is the result of perseverance, strategic thinking, and an unwavering commitment to one's vision. The journey is long, often arduous, filled with obstacles that test the mettle of even the most determined visionaries. There is no such thing as the other side or 9 to 5 till you are in your pursuit.

In driving global economic growth and job creation, the role of entrepreneurs and intrapreneurs is indispensable. In startups, the entrepreneurs are the catalysts in the economy, initiating new businesses that create jobs and stimulate further economic development. In corporations, intrapreneurs bring disruptive technologies or methodologies, sparking innovation within established industries.

There are ecosystems supporting these journeys – from the network of investors, accelerators, and mentors in the startup world to the resources, guidance, and support structures within corporations. Both are vital in helping these ventures flourish.

The path of entrepreneurship, whether in a startup or a corporate setting, is laden with as many challenges as there are opportunities. While the challenges are significant, the opportunities for innovation, personal growth, and making a tangible impact are equally substantial. We grapple with securing funding, assembling effective teams, crafting sustainable business models, and navigating intricate legal and regulatory landscapes in startups.

In corporations, the challenge lies in pushing innovative ideas through the layers of corporate structure and aligning them with the broader organisational goals. Often picking up suboptimal alternatives over the ideal ones just because they are better aligned with corporate objectives. The environments of startup and corporate entrepreneurship are characterised by rapid change and evolution. In both startup and corporate entrepreneurship, adaptability isn't just a trait; it's a necessity for survival and success. We must be adaptable, ready to pivot our strategies in response to market feedback and continuous learning. This dynamic nature demands an ongoing evolution and a keen ability to stay ahead.

It doesn't matter if you are navigating the untested waters of a startup or steering through the complex dynamics of a corporate giant, entrepreneurship is a journey of courage, resilience, and transformation, reserved for those who dare to dream and are relentless in making those dreams a reality.

Why This Book, and Why Now?

In the world of startups, where technology often takes the spotlight, this book emerges as a transformative guide, placing a crucial yet often overlooked aspect at its heart: the power of selling benefits over features. Experiencing it first-hand, as a technical expert, I observed a disparity between successful and unsuccessful uptake by the end consumer on various technology products. This observation led me to highlight this issue with the view to provide this as a resource for every aspiring entrepreneur on an often-overlooked perspective that can make a significant difference in the outcome:

A Focus Beyond Features, to Benefits

While features are essential, this book illuminates why benefits should take centre stage. It's about resonating with consumers and investors alike by highlighting how your startup can enrich their lives or solve their problems. This approach shifts the focus from what your product or service does to how it makes a difference.

Practical, Applied with Examples

Designed as an agile toolkit rather than a linear narrative, this book encourages you to dive into sections that align with your current challenges, apply the insights, and witness the impact unfold in real-time. It's about action, not just theory.

Flexible Learning and Application

The benefit of this book lies in its flexibility. It invites you to revisit, relearn, and reimplement its teachings as your entrepreneurial journey evolves. Each aspect is brief with ideas that can help transform knowledge into tangible outcomes.

Guidance and Reasoning - Every Step of the Way

This book offers practical examples to supplement your entrepreneurial journey. Whether you're brainstorming your next big idea or navigating a critical decision, this book is there to guide you.

| 2 |

Approach to Startup Journey

Embracing a Benefit-Centric Approach

When it comes to startups, I come across a large array of technical founders. They truly enjoy what they do, however in the process of doing so they fall in love with their product so much that they often forget the benefit it brings to the consumer who will eventually buy the product and help establish a thriving business. Hence, my endeavour to talk about embracing a benefit-centric approach. This method ensures a deeper connection with customers and a more sustainable business model. My quick take on why I have found the benefit-centric approach being integral to success:

1. **Business with a Focus on Customer:** in the journey of entrepreneurship, numerous components such as market opportunity identification, product or service development, team building, and growth planning are involved. A benefit-centric approach ensures these elements are addressed with a focus on the benefits they offer to customers, not just the features they boast. This helps in creating offerings that resonate deeply with the market's

6

needs and desires alongside ensuring an offer is well timed in the market - a key driver of success.[1]

2. **Customer-Oriented Strategy:** this method allows entrepreneurs to craft a cohesive and integrated strategy that revolves around the benefits their business offers. It ensures all aspects of the business are harmoniously aligned with the core value proposition, leading to a stronger market position and more meaningful customer relationships.

3. **Customer-Centric Solutions:** understanding and prioritising customer benefits aid in identifying potential risks associated with market acceptance and competition. This focus on customer satisfaction and value creation is critical in navigating and overcoming startup challenges and obstacles effectively.

4. **Sustainable and Scalable Model Focused on Long-Term Value:** by centering the business model on customer benefits, entrepreneurs can establish a more sustainable and scalable venture. This ensures the business grows in both size and value as it continues to meet and exceed expectations. This also shifts the focus on creation of traction and revenue, early profitability and creation of a customer funded business. Even if you, as a founder, need to raise money you are likely to be in a better bargaining power.

Benefit-Centric Startup Methodology

In the journey of startup development, a benefit-centric methodology involves a thorough understanding and addressing of several key components, all viewed through the lens of how they deliver benefits to the customer. These components include:

- Identifying Market Needs, with a Focus on Benefits: the initial step involves conducting market research to understand potential customers' needs and preferences. You just need to get out of the room. There is no such thing as desk research in this business. Evaluate the market gaps in terms of benefits, not just features. Key questions to ask yourself:

- ○ What problem are you solving in terms of benefits?
- ○ Why are you choosing to solve this problem?
- ○ Who exactly are you solving it for, and what benefits will they receive?
- ○ Are you addressing a real need or are you infatuated with your own idea?
- ○ What if you can visualise the idea perfectly but cannot address a need because people might not know now that they need it?

- Developing a Product or Service, Centred on Benefits: upon identifying market needs, develop a product or service that fulfills these needs through tangible benefits. Craft a value proposition focused on how the product or service enriches the customer's life.

- Creating a Business Plan with a Benefit Perspective: draft a business plan that outlines your mission, goals, and strategies, all rooted in delivering customer benefits. Include financial viability. This needs to be numbers that you expect... and why. Your assumptions are more important than actual numbers because if numbers are incorrect without any assumptions your projections will be super vague at best. Once you can work on underpinning assumptions, fixing the numbers becomes a much easier task.

- Building a Team of Associates, Alliances, Partners or Co-founders - Aligned with the 'Benefit Vision': assemble a team that understands and shares the vision of providing customer benefits. Building a startup is more than a job, it is buying into and working on a vision. Without buy-in, you are gearing for its failure. Include employees, advisers, mentors, and stakeholders who can contribute to this benefit-focused approach.

- Launching, with an Emphasis on Customer Benefits: introduce your product or service to the market with a clear message of the benefits it offers. Develop a launch plan that spotlights how your offering enhances customer experiences or solves problems effectively.

With benefit-centric methodology, entrepreneurs can ensure that every aspect of their startup is aligned with delivering real value to their customers. This holistic view not only increases the chances of startup success but also fosters deeper customer engagement and loyalty.

Benefit-Driven Company Culture in Startups

As a founder, the culture you cultivate within your startup transcends the confines of your office walls. It is, indeed, the very essence of your value proposition, shaping the way your business delivers benefits and experiences to your customers. Let's talk about how a well-nurtured, benefit-focused company culture can be a strategic cornerstone impacting every facet of business - from product development to the nuances of customer engagement.

Embedding Customer-Centric Values

The journey to a benefit-driven culture begins with embedding customer-centric values deep into your company's core. This process involves fostering a mindset throughout your organisation where every decision, innovation, or customer interaction is evaluated based on the value it brings to your customers. Once the company's culture is deeply rooted in understanding and prioritising the needs and preferences of your customers, it naturally leads to the creation of products and services that not only meet these needs but also deliver truly memorable experiences. The question that needs to be asked here is how does this benefit our customer?

Innovation and Creativity in Benefit Delivery

Central to this culture is a spirit of innovation and creativity, pivotal in perpetually enhancing how benefits are delivered to your customers. This requires encouraging a team to think outside the box and embrace experimentation can lead to ground-breaking ideas, significantly elevating the customer experience. Imagine a culture where your team members are constantly encouraged to view challenges from the customer's perspective – this can lead to innovative solutions that markedly boost user satisfaction.

Aligning Team Efforts Towards Customer Satisfaction

In a benefit-centric culture, every individual in your team, from the product developers to the marketing strategists, understands their role in enhancing customer satisfaction. Such alignment ensures collective efforts are focused on a singular goal – maximising the benefits delivered to your customers. For instance, customer service teams in this culture are more than just problem solvers; they become the voice of your customers, offering valuable insights that can inform product refinements or inspire new services.

Building a Brand Synonymous with Customer Benefits

Your company's culture often mirrors itself in your brand's image. A startup grounded in a culture that prioritises delivering customer benefits can cultivate a brand associated with trust, quality, and customer satisfaction. This aids in retaining existing customers and attracts new ones drawn to your brand's commitment to prioritising their needs.

Sustainable Growth and Customer Loyalty

A culture driven by delivering tangible benefits fosters sustainable business growth and customer loyalty. When customers consistently receive real value and positive experiences, it cultivates loyalty and encourages word-of-mouth referrals, leading to a loyal customer base, repeat business, and sustained growth over time.

Employee Engagement and Retention

Nurturing a culture that emphasises delivering customer benefits also positively influences your team. Witnessing the direct impact of their efforts on customers enhances job satisfaction, morale and engagement among employees, leading to higher retention rates and attracting talent passionate about contributing to a customer-focused environment.

Adapting to Market Changes with Agility

Startups with a robust benefit-driven culture are also more adept at adapting to market changes. By staying attuned to customer feedback and market trends, such companies can pivot or modify their offerings more adeptly, continuing to deliver the benefits their customers have come to expect.

Instilling a benefit-driven culture in your startup is a fundamental pillar for success in today's competitive landscape. It influences how you develop your offerings, how you interact with your customers, and how you position your startup in the market. By fostering such a culture, you do more than meet customer expectations – you exceed them, thereby solidifying your startup's position as a leader in your industry.

| 3 |

Essential Questions to ask yourself

"Knowing yourself is the beginning of all wisdom." - Aristotle

Most founders itch for a great idea and whilst it certainly can help, embarking on the entrepreneurial path demands more than just a ground-breaking idea; it requires a deep understanding of the unique benefits your startup will offer and how they resonate with your target audience. How are you going to create value by flawless execution, and how will you appropriate value?

In the modern-day entrepreneurship, where the emphasis is shifting towards creating value and memorable experiences, it is essential to align every facet of your startup with this benefit-centric mindset.

After spending time with a number of founders over the last many years and filtering the successful ones, I have highlighted the following 25 questions to guide aspiring entrepreneurs through a self-assessment journey. They represent critical checkpoints on your path to building a startup that genuinely understands and delivers on its promise of benefits and experiences to customers. By pondering these questions, you will gain insights into the core of what makes a startup thrive in today's competitive market, ensuring that your venture is ready to launch and primed to make a significant and beneficial impact in the lives of your customers.

1. How does my business idea uniquely benefit potential customers? I know many founders have not spoken to their prospective customers. Often, they don't even know who might be a prospective customer.

2. Have I conducted market research that focuses on the benefits sought by my target audience? Founders often work on a hunch, they have come across someone in the past who indicated a problem, or they themselves have been in an industry long enough to assume that a problem exists. The problems should be sharp and crisply defined, otherwise it is very hard to penetrate a well-established market.

3. Do I understand the experiential needs and preferences of my target market? The market may be an overcrowded space, where it is increasingly harder for people to exist without being pushed around by others who have taken the nice 'corner spots'. If the market is not crowded, it simply would suggest no one is there yet or no one will ever get there as it is not big or profitable enough. While you may need to know the needs and preferences of the market you should also question if it is worth the pursuit for a few decades.

4. What unique benefits does my value proposition offer that set me apart from competitors? Sometimes it may not need to be too unique in all the aspects of the value proposition, just one or two differentiators is enough. For example, in a market where everyone can deliver food at home, freshly made warm meals allowed for Uber to become an easy differentiator.

5. Does my business prioritise customer benefits and experiences? As mentioned above, you may be offering the same as everyone else; sometimes uncovering a particular aspect of customer benefit can make a big difference.

6. Have I included a focus on customer benefits in my business plan? This should start with your mindset, often we fall in love with what we have to offer, to the point that we forget one main idea - what we are creating can only have one beneficiary: our customer and our purpose is to turn a great idea into a phenomenal business that our target market falls in love with. The first sale certainly happens to the founder as they have to love their offering, but it should be done with the sole focus being on customers.

7. Am I aware of how legal and regulatory frameworks impact customer benefits in my industry? What you may be offering to the market or customers may have legal implications. It may be unlawful to sell in certain areas. You may have something great to offer, but unless you follow the legal framework it can be personally challenging for your business and yourself.

8. Have I explored funding sources that align with delivering high-quality customer benefits? Funding sources may have their own agenda, or they may have a clear focus on domains and technologies that may or may not align with the benefits you may ought to deliver to your customers. Your investors may come from domains where they may not understand your market or the benefits. This misalignment may be overlooked out of urgency or desperation to raise funds but can impact your focus in short, medium or long term.

9. Is my revenue generation strategy centred around the benefits provided to customers? Everyone wanting to start the game of startups wants to get a lot of revenue very quickly. Most forget

that the network effects and word of mouth are among the fastest drivers to capture new customers. To create network effect and word of mouth, the cardinal principle is to offer immense value in exchange for what customers feel is a 'bargain', a belief that they are then willing to share with others.

10. Have I assessed risks in my ability to deliver consistent benefits to customers? Markets are ever changing. You can get customers with immense value and often do so by enticing them with marketing, or giving offers that they simply can't deny. After a point in time the benefit you offer to them must be compelling enough to sustain their ongoing interest.

11. Does my team have the mindset and skills to prioritise customer benefits? Pack a bunch of nerds or specialists in a room and they will start bragging about their expertise. I have been an expert so have seen this first-hand. At the end of the day what matters is how you are perceived by those who want to rent your nerdiness or expertise. When it comes to customers, how your expertise translates into benefits for them should be your focus.

12. Have I sought partners and advisers who understand the importance of customer experience? Talk is cheap, it is the action that is the most expensive element in a startup. Many advisors may have sound advice to offer, but sadly they do not step out of their own room to understand where the world is heading. When you want to learn you should expand your circle and open-mindedness, so that you are absorbing input from a number of people and perspectives. It can quickly become overwhelming as everyone has a perspective. The trick is you take all in and keep what is relevant and park the rest away for the future. Consider yourself to have a repository of inputs which you can reach out to on a need's basis.

13. Do I possess or am planning to acquire skills specifically for enhancing customer benefits? Asking the right question is the key. Customers want the benefit of arriving earlier at their destination than it was possible, however often they cannot look into the future so framing the question around benefits or the 'what' rather than the 'how' makes a key difference.

14. How will I manage my time to ensure a focus on delivering and improving customer benefits? Everything comes with a trade-off. You can focus on optimising the workflow in the startup, recruiting the best talent, meeting potential suppliers or just on delivering and improving benefits to the customer.

15. Do I have a support network that values a benefit-focused approach? Many organisations and startups suffer from 'group-think'. Looking at a benefit focussed approach may need challenging or questioning the norm. Do you have a network within and outside the organisation that encourages and supports a benefit centric approach?

16. How will I balance commitments while ensuring a consistent customer experience? When the time pressure is high, and the deadlines are tight we often lose the objectivity of why we are in the business in the first place. We forget our commitments towards meaningful customer experience centred around benefits we ought to deliver.

17. What is my strategy for overcoming setbacks in delivering customer benefits? While you shift your focus on customer benefits, staff may think they are being ignored or secondary, which may lead to internal conflicts. There may be cost imperatives. You need to come up with the process of engaging with and observing customers, without being intrusive.

18. How will my business positively impact the environment and society in terms of benefits? By adopting sustainable practices and focusing on social responsibility, how can we reduce our carbon footprint and waste? How can we design products that promote energy efficiency and recyclability? Consider how creating local jobs and providing fair wages can uplift communities. Reflect on the impact of ethical supply chains and community engagement in promoting a healthier planet and a more equitable society. How can these efforts ensure long-term environmental and societal benefits?

19. What are my plans for scaling up the benefits and experiences my business offers? How can we leverage technology and innovation to enhance customer experiences? What strategies can we employ to expand our reach while maintaining high-quality service? Consider partnerships, new markets, and continuous feedback to refine and scale our offerings. How will investing in talent and resources drive growth and ensure sustained customer satisfaction?

20. Have I considered how potential exit strategies will affect the benefits provided to customers? How can we ensure a smooth transition that maintains or enhances customer benefits? What measures can be taken to preserve service quality and continuity? Reflect on how different exit strategies might impact customer relationships and satisfaction. How will we communicate changes effectively to reassure and retain our customer base?

21. Do I have financial resources to sustain a business that delivers high-quality benefits? I am sure you have heard about the FFFF approach to seeking initial money for a startup. This usually refers to: Founder, Friends, Family and Fools. The first three are obvious; you may be questioning where the fool got the money from. The reason the fourth category of investor is called a Fool is because they make the investment in you on an emotional

basis. They don't care about your venture, but they want you to succeed so they will be there for you and invest in you. From an investment point of view that may not be the best decision. I recall someone I know very well, having invested heavily in movies where his nephew was playing a lead role. The movies were not successful at the box office, but it did not prevent him from his continued investment.

22. How will I manage finances to continuously enhance the benefits offered? The reasonable period for which you will need to raise funds can typically vary, however 9 months or so is good and in case of bridging rounds it can be defined by the situation. Be prepared as it can take longer than you anticipate. Your network can always help you to reach out to the right investors and for subsequent rounds your existing investors may be able to refer you. Most importantly if you are doing well and creating something of value, people will seek you out and like to be a part of your journey.

23. Is my vision for the business centred around the long-term benefits to customers? Your offer may be the new bright shiny object; however, you must be mindful that customer interests will change over time, and they will continue to look for a brighter and shinier object. You will need to constantly pivot and change. You must have a vision for the long term without losing sight of the next best thing that you can offer to customers.

24. Have I set goals that are measurable in terms of customer satisfaction and benefit delivery? How happy are your customers? It is customary to measure the net promoter score. There will always be a certain bias underlying your calculations: customers that provide you with feedback are usually selected by your business, or self-selected. Business-selected feedback is often skewed positive, whilst self-selected are either very happy or very annoyed. The true measure of customer satisfaction is tapping into 100%

of your customers. This may not be practical in all cases but is the best alternative. Continuously listen to your customers, and the challenges they face.

25. Am I prepared to take calculated risks to innovate and enhance customer benefits? At every stage of a startup, one is challenged by trade-offs. That also means taking well informed and calculated risks that eventually result in customer benefits.

| 4 |

Building The Mindset

"Whether you think you can, or you think you can't - you're right." - Henry Ford

Mind Over Matter – It Truly Does Matter

The only difference between a founder starting out and an unemployed person is the passion, the zeal, the energy and the enthusiasm that a founder has and the ways the eyes light up in the pursuit of something new, something different, something to call their own. That is what will compound in the long term.

Welcome to this world of startups. As you embark on your journey in the world of startups, or on your journey as an entrepreneur, you will realise that the core of a successful startup is not always a ground-breaking idea or cutting-edge technology but is in your mindset as a founder.

An idea that goes from strategy to execution to a product that the customers hopefully cherish and enjoy on a sustained basis and the rents or profits exceed the cost in the long run. As a founder you will find that this journey is not instant. It can take days, weeks, months, years or decades. What the world sees is what is visible: the outcome, not the challenges you have gone through.

Your responsibility, as a startup founder, thus lies into preparing yourself for this journey. Realising that overnight success may be decades away. Thus, you can cultivate a mindset that transcends your current capabilities and limitations, to develop a resilience to deal with the challenges that come your way. Expanding the mindset is crucial in steering your startup towards success. Resources are always secondary.

The Founder's Mindset

Startups, often extensions of a founder(s) vision and skills, are intimately tied to their founder's abilities and perspectives. Often when few founders get together, magic happens. There is a large array of companies where founders got together through serendipity like in the case of Airbnb, Canva, Apple, Google amongst many others; suddenly the growth curve became exponential. You should never discount who you are with. There are many startup carcasses out there that did not make it, due to founders not being on the same page. I don't want you to be part of the same statistic. The growth trajectory of your startup is intrinsically linked to your personal and professional development which is going to be in sync.

Mastery Over Your Own Mind

Perhaps the only way you can master your mind is by continuous and voracious learning. This is not about knowledge to action. You may think you are competing with others; however, your primary competition is always going to be the person in the mirror, and a pursuit of being better, every moment. Perhaps you will need to embrace the process of learning new skills and gaining diverse experiences. This will either help you enhance business acumen or sharpen problem-solving. It could be your leadership skills or interpersonal skills. You will note that every new skill will equip you better for the challenges ahead. A word of caution here that learning is not about knowledge accumulation; it's about its decisive application; be agile to pivot and change when course correction is needed along your journey.

Developing a Growth Mindset

Cultivate a growth mindset, the belief that abilities and intelligence can be developed through dedication and hard work. This mindset empowers you to view challenges as opportunities for growth rather than insurmountable obstacles.

Navigating Setbacks with Resilience

Understand that setbacks are an inevitable part of the startup journey. Develop resilience to persevere through these challenges, viewing them as opportunities to learn and evolve. Trust me, it is easier said than done - I have heard a founder say that his overnight success took him fifteen years.

Embracing Change and Uncertainty

The startup landscape is dynamic and ever-changing. Adapting and evolving with these changes is crucial. Learn to thrive in uncertainty, making informed decisions even in the most unpredictable situations.

Continuous Personal and Professional Growth

Recognise that leading a startup is a journey of profound personal growth. Pushing out of your comfort zone is not just a necessity but a norm in this journey. Strive to be the best version of yourself, constantly evolving to meet the demands of a rapidly changing world.

Your growth is not just confined to business metrics; it's a holistic journey encompassing personal development, resilience, and adaptability. Embracing this expansive mindset is not a choice but a necessity to navigate the complex terrain of startups and make a meaningful impact.

Acknowledge That Everything Starts with Mind Over Matter

Our ego or arrogance may not allow us to acknowledge that when we are successful, we attribute our success to hard work, and when unsuccessful we blame much of it on bad luck. Though the truth may be somewhere in between, much starts from our imagination. Our ideas are conceived in our head and hearts before they are created in the real world. Having a vivid picture in our mind or mind clarity helps us refine it in the real world.

Entrepreneurs have succeeded with a strong vision and a growth mindset. They have held an unwavering faith and focus on their goals with a willingness to learn and adapt. That said, often every story has a backstory hidden from the limelight, so you don't have to take everything that you read, hear, or see as sacrosanct. The other key theme you should always keep in mind is that by venturing into a startup, you are creating a business. Having clarity on this one simple idea is paramount for success. Some outstanding names that I am personally in awe of are:

Steve Jobs, the co-founder of Apple Inc., who is known for his strong vision and relentless pursuit of excellence, which helped him lead Apple to become one of the most successful and innovative companies in the world. Despite facing numerous challenges and setbacks, including being fired from his own company, Jobs never lost sight of his vision and was able to overcome his own limitations and lead Apple to success. Focus has been a key. However, he has also been a proponent of learning and being hungry for knowledge ("stay hungry, stay foolish" - Steve Jobs) as often we are able to connect the dots when we look back. I believe it is the cross domain intelligence that brings new perspectives, along with focus that puts us into a unique and advantageous position to create something completely different and new.

Elon Musk, the CEO of SpaceX and Tesla, who is known for his ambitious and forward-thinking approach, which has helped him push the boundaries of technology and entrepreneurship. It seems to me that he faces numerous challenges and setbacks almost every day. Despite the failure of several rockets and the near collapse of Tesla, Musk has been able to maintain a growth mindset and continue to grow his companies and pursue his vision.

A less well-known example is Sara Blakely, the founder of Spanx. Blakely started her company with just $5,000 in savings and no experience in the fashion industry. Through her determination and resourcefulness, she was able to grow her company into a successful and innovative brand. Blakely attributes her success to her willingness to learn and adapt to new challenges.

To draw a parallel between the three or the hundreds of others who are successful, it is their mindset which sets them apart. With the right mindset you are bound to reach your destination, sooner or later.

Craziness Index: Are Founders Crazy or Is the Rest of the World Crazy

Most entrepreneurs are considered 'crazy' because of their ways of thinking. They are often misunderstood by all around them. You should not feel bad if your partner, sibling or family does not fully support or understand your idea. This happens because entrepreneurs are used to thinking outside the box or living in the future and challenging conventional wisdom. Entrepreneurs who are willing to take risks and think in unconventional ways are seen as 'crazy' by others who are more risk-averse and conservative.

Elon Musk, the CEO of SpaceX and Tesla, is often considered 'crazy' by some because of his ambitious and unconventional approach to business. Musk has pursued numerous projects that are considered risky or difficult, such as developing reusable rockets and creating a network of underground tunnels. Despite facing numerous challenges and setbacks, Musk has continued to pursue them with a relentless focus and determination.

Jeff Bezos, the founder and CEO of Amazon is known for his long-term thinking and his willingness to make bold bets. Some of those initiatives did not pay off for many years (and many failed as well). He invested heavily in Amazon's cloud computing business, even though it was not immediately profitable. He has also pursued other projects considered risky or difficult, such as developing delivery drones, seen as 'crazy' by some, but they have helped Amazon become one of the most successful and innovative companies in the world.

Richard Branson, the founder of Virgin Group, is known for his adventurous and unconventional approach to business. He has started more than 400 companies in a wide range of industries, including air travel, music, and space exploration. Branson's willingness to take risks and pursue ambitious projects has earned him a reputation as a 'crazy' entrepreneur, but it has also helped him to achieve success and make a significant impact on the world.

Peter Thiel, the co-founder of PayPal and Palantir, is known for his contrarian and thought-provoking approach to business. He has made several bold investments, including early bets on companies like Facebook and Airbnb, and has challenged conventional wisdom on issues such as higher education and the future of technology. Thiel's 'crazy' ideas and approach to entrepreneurship have helped him to achieve success and shape the direction of the tech industry.

If you are considered crazy, then you might be just right to start a new venture.

Corporate Entrepreneurship Is Often a Challenge

Corporations often value conformity and following established ways of doing things, while startups are known for their innovative thinking and willingness to challenge the status quo. This can sometimes make it difficult for corporate entrepreneurship initiatives to succeed, as they may face resistance from within the organisation due to a lack of alignment with the company's traditional ways of working.

This doesn't mean that corporate entrepreneurship is always doomed to fail. Many successful companies have been able to foster a culture of innovation and entrepreneurship, even within a larger corporate structure. It just takes a commitment to supporting and promoting these types of initiatives, as well as a willingness to take risks and embrace change. The best way I have seen this tackled is to have a buy into this paradigm from the senior leadership and create a separate incubation environment within the organisation.

The Trap of a Loved One's Opinions

You cannot offer others benefits if you are not the beneficiary of your own mindset. It is easy to fall into the trap of seeking input from family and friends when it comes to your startup. You may trust them and have always sought advice from them in the past. Unfortunately, if they are not objective or lack the necessary expertise and experience to provide useful input about your business, their advice may be driven more by emotions than practicality. They don't want you or your business to fail, and as a result, they may support you even when you're on the wrong path. They mean well, but their advice might not always be helpful. Think of it this way: seeking business advice from friends and family is like asking a lawyer for heart surgery advice or requesting noodles at McDonald's.

Your family and friends may bring their personal biases into the conversation, or they might try to emotionally support you by saying what is safe and comforting. This can lead to decisions that are not in the best interest of the business and may ultimately hinder its growth and success.

Seeking input from family and friends can create conflicts of interest, as they may not always prioritise the founder's best interests. For example, if you seek input from your spouse on a business decision, they might be more concerned with your personal well-being than with the success of the business. This can lead to conflicts and misunderstandings that can harm the business or become a cause of relationship disaster.

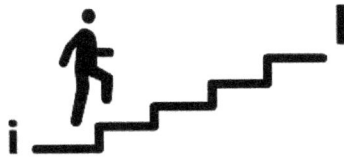

Mental growth, grows our identity i --> I
image credit - Sameer Babbar

When we go through mental growth, our identity changes, and this can be difficult for people around us. We go through the process of expanding our knowledge, skills and abilities, gaining new perspectives on the world. We learn new things, gain new experiences, and develop new ways of thinking.

People around us react because they may be used to our old identity and may not know how to relate to our new, magnified identity.

When you go through a period of mental growth and learn to think more critically and independently, you may develop new beliefs and values that are different from those of your friends and family. Your friends and family members, who may be used to your old beliefs and values and may not know how to relate to your new beliefs and values.

When you go through a period of mental growth and gain new skills and abilities, you may become more confident and assertive, those around you, who may be used to your old, less confident and assertive identity and may not know how to respond to your new, more confident and assertive identity.

It is important for us to be aware of this, and to communicate openly with those around us about our growth and how it is affecting our identity during the process of growth. This can help to bridge the gap between our old and new identities and make the transition smoother for everyone.

| 5 |

Magnifying Your Identity: You... But Better

"Create a better version of yourself. You will spend a lot
of time together with yourself." - Sameer Babbar

Your journey as a founder will lead you through personal and professional growth. The growth results in magnifying your identity.

Develop a Strong Personal Brand

A strong personal brand can help you to stand out from the competition and to build your reputation as a thought leader in your industry. This involves defining your own unique value proposition, identifying your target audience, and creating a consistent and compelling message that resonates with that audience. It can be a great way for you to increase their visibility and credibility, which can in turn lead to more opportunities for your business. Here are some steps to develop a strong personal brand:

1. Define your brand: start by thinking about what makes you unique and what sets you apart from other founders in your

industry. This could be your values, your expertise, or your experiences. Use this to develop a clear and compelling brand message that can be consistently communicated across all your channels. Leverage your uniqueness as there is only one you. If you copy others, take permission and make sure you attribute... even when it comes to simple ideas. The ones you copy can become your sources of referral if you do it the right way.

2. Identify your target audience: next, think about who you want to reach with your personal brand. This could be potential customers, investors, media outlets, or other key stakeholders. Having a clear idea of your target audience will help you tailor your messaging and content to resonate with them.

3. Establish a presence online: in today's world, having an online presence is essential for building a personal brand. This can include creating a website or blog, being active on social media, and contributing to online discussions and forums related to your industry. Social media, content creators and influencers may play a key role, taking your message to your target audience

4. Create valuable content: one of the best ways to build a personal brand is to consistently create and share valuable content. This could be through writing articles, creating videos, sharing insights on social media, or speaking at events. The key is to focus on providing value and solving problems for your target audience.

5. Steer clear of 'free': it is the fastest way to undermine your own potential. You have limited time in life and if someone expects your time or your possessions for free, it is a sign of disrespect. They are simply telling you that they either don't respect you or don't respect themselves. There can of course be another cause: that they cannot afford to pay you just yet. You must exercise your discretion if you are paying it forward, doing a pro-bono job, demonstrating your offering, opening a door or being sent on a wild goose chase. You don't want a client who does not have intent or potential to pay you.

6. Build relationships and collaborate: building a personal brand is not just about promoting yourself, it's also about building relationships and collaborating with others. Attend industry events, join professional organisations, and seek out opportunities to work with others in your field. This can help you expand your network and raise your visibility.

Some examples of founders who have successfully built personal brands include Tim Ferris and Gary Vaynerchuk. These founders have incorporated a combination of the above steps to establish themselves as thought leaders in their respective industries and build strong personal brands.

Network

Networking and building relationships with other industry leaders, investors, and influencers can help you gain visibility and credibility, as well as access new opportunities and resources. This can involve attending industry events, joining relevant organisations, and leveraging social media and other digital platforms to connect with others. A strong network can provide valuable connections, support, and advice, which can be instrumental in helping you grow your business. Here are some steps you can take to build a strong network of relationships, even if you have limited experience:

1. Identify your goals: before you start networking, it's important to have a clear idea of what you want to achieve. Do you want to meet potential customers, investors, partners, or mentors? Knowing your goals will help you focus your efforts and make the most of your networking opportunities.

2. Seek out networking opportunities: there are many ways to meet potential connections, including attending industry events, joining professional organisations, or participating in online forums and discussion groups. Look for opportunities that align with your goals and make the most of them by being proactive and engaging with others.

3. Be authentic and transparent: as a founder with no track record, it's important to be authentic and transparent about your experiences and your goals. Be open about where you are in your journey and what you're trying to achieve and be willing to listen and learn from others. This can help build trust and establish credibility.

4. Provide value: to build strong relationships, you need to be a valuable connection for others. This means being willing to help others and share your expertise, as well as being open to new opportunities and introductions. By providing value, you'll be more likely to build strong, lasting relationships. Remember relationships are always two-way streets.

5. Nurture your relationships: building a strong network is not just about making initial connections, it's also about nurturing those relationships over time. Stay in touch with your connections and continue to provide value and support. This can help you build deeper, more meaningful relationships and expand your network.

Some examples of founders who have built strong networks despite having no track record include Mark Zuckerberg, who founded Facebook while still a student at Harvard, and Jan Koum, who co-founded WhatsApp without any prior tech industry experience.

Word of caution: no amount of networking is a substitute for outcome. As Charlie Munger emphasised that true success comes from delivering unparalleled value and results, which naturally attracts people, rather than relying solely on networking or other superficial tactics.

Be Authentic and Transparent

Being authentic and transparent can help you build trust and credibility with your audience and differentiate yourself from others in your industry. This involves being open and honest about your experiences, challenges, and successes, and being willing to share your thoughts and insights with others. It can be challenging for you to appear authentic and transparent if you're not feeling that way on the inside. However, there are some steps you can take to position yourself in a way that appears authentic and transparent, even if you're not feeling that way:

1. Be genuine: the most important thing is to be genuine in your interactions with others. Don't try to fake authenticity or transparency, as this can come across as insincere and can damage your relationships. Instead, focus on being genuine and honest in your communication, and let your true personality shine through. For example, some founders might manipulate numbers to appear more attractive to investors. While this strategy might work in the short term, it has the potential to damage credibility in the long run.

2. Be open and vulnerable: authenticity and transparency often involve being open and vulnerable. Don't be afraid to share your struggles and challenges, as this can help build trust and make others more likely to connect with you. Everyone who has achieved something has had their fair share of struggles.

3. Practice self-awareness: one of the key components of authenticity is self-awareness. Take the time to reflect on your thoughts, feelings, and motivations, and be honest with yourself about who you are and what you stand for. This can help you better understand yourself and be more authentic and transparent in your interactions with others.

4. Be consistent: authenticity and transparency involve consistency in your actions and your words. Be consistent in your behaviour and your messaging, and make sure that your actions align with your values and your brand.

5. Seek feedback: seek feedback from others on how you come across. Ask for honest feedback from your network and use it to continue improving and refining your authenticity and transparency.

Be a Thought Leader

You need to become a thought leader to establish yourself as an expert and gain recognition and respect from others. Social media is driving people's attention. Perhaps, depending on your skill and focus, you may consider writing articles, blog posts, speaking at conferences or events, sharing your insights and expertise through social media or other digital platforms. Being a thought leader is a valuable way to increase visibility and credibility, perhaps you are known to the target market before you reach out to them, which is certainly a way to grow the business. In other ways it is 'pull-driven' and not 'push-driven'. They reach out to you knowing that you have value to offer. Some key steps you can consider working on are

1. Defining your expertise: you need to be super clear on this, who you are and what you stand for. You may have liked to lean on your qualifications, job, or title but always remember that is your past. You are not going to your past, but to the future.
In the era where people change careers so many times in their life, allow yourself to position yourself as an expert in the field. But you, make sure it is deep expertise. You don't want people to rapidly abandon you because there is a better version of you. Don't copy the ideas without attributing the original creator as those who are well read will call it a 'con'. Attribution will still

end up positioning you among the thought leaders even though an idea is not yours. Many have established themselves as experts by professing the ideas of others.

You should not try to be everything to everyone; instead, aim to provide value for a specific audience. You can explore an industry, topic or problem and bring your own unique perspective to the approach. Network is important but overrated. If you are truly creating something of value, your network will emerge.

2. Establish a presence online: In today's world, if you are not online, your professional and personal existence may be questioned. Often, you may need to justify your absence from social media platforms. Hence your digital footprint is vital. For example, when I publish my blog online it reaches thousands of readers. Your audience must know what you stand for. That is the essence of who you are. That is what positions you as a thought leader. If you find it hard to get started, you can consider sharing your views on a topic, until you get your mental muscle ready for your own content. Please remember, you cannot become a thought leader by being negative or cynical about what others have to say, but you must put your own perspective. Thought leaders have value because they have their own constructive perspectives, and they add value.

3. Create valuable content: your content must be of value. Avoid recycling content without adding your own context and perspective, and always provide attribution when using other people's ideas. Bring value so people can reach out to you, with the view that there is more where 'that' came from. The key is to focus on providing value and solving problems for your target audience.

4. Network and collaborate: you need to go beyond self-promotion to building genuine relationships and collaborating with others. Your success is likely to be more sustainable if everyone around you also benefits from your expertise and knowledge. If you

become a catalyst of benefit and success for others, you will be sought out, invited by others to work and to raise your visibility. Often being associated with industry giants can enhance your visibility significantly.

5. Measure and refine: You need to constantly evaluate, measure and track how you are progressing in your journey. Monitor web traffic, incoming calls, and inquiries to assess how effectively you are capturing the attention of your target audience.

Take Risks and Innovate

As a founder you will take risks for the rest of us. It is more than likely that you may have to take the fall. Your strength is going to be your ability to get up and get going again. As a founder you must take money risk carefully as it comes with significant trust. Sometimes managing investment money (often poorly) and not focusing on generating revenue becomes part of an unnecessary risk a startup must carry. Innovation is no longer enough. Now founders have started caring about the pace of innovation. Many startups are carefully listening to feedback, and constantly improving and releasing the updated versions of software daily. It's important to take calculated risks and minimise, mitigate, or migrate risk, whenever possible.

Risk Management Matrix
Creative Commons

1. Identify the risks: running a startup is a risk. A significant number of startups fail. A significant number of established businesses fail. The rewards of a business that becomes successful are huge as well. You can identify the risks by observing others who have failed or succeeded, the book that you are holding will give you a glimpse into an array of risks but will not solve them for you. You can't avoid risks, but you can take calculated steps to identify, minimise, mitigate, and manage the risks. The first step in taking calculated risks is to identify the risks involved in each situation. Take the time to thoroughly assess the potential risks, their likelihood and their impact.

2. Develop a risk management plan: once you have identified the risks, you need to think through how you are going to manage them. It could be a data leak, an unhappy employee, or a change of law. You cannot anticipate everything that can go wrong, but you could always anticipate and have strategies for dealing with problems. Consider this as diversifying your investment, hedging your bets, or having a contingency plan. You cannot control what happens around you, but you can plan and control your reaction to it.

3. Monitor and update your plan: you will need to revisit risks that you are anticipating and how you are going to address them on a regular basis. Companies might face lawsuits as competitors try to divert their marketing budgets into legal battles, stalling their growth. Many established companies can lawyer up, while the small startup may be thwarted. Often it pays to navigate under the radar while you reach sizable proportions. Often, this is the reason why one may need a cornerstone investor or a VC fund with deep pockets. There is a greater chance you will be backed by them if you are not in default, rather than going alone.

4. Be prepared to adapt: at times you are unable to minimise, mitigate or migrate your risk. You may need to adapt or pivot. Often a large business may release a feature that you find hard to compete with and may cause threat to your existence. Perhaps going to the drawing board and looking at how you can recover from the current stalemate and move in a new direction. Every step will have uncertainty, as there is a likely chance it was an unexplored path.

5. Communicate with stakeholders: talk. Make sure to communicate with stakeholders about your risk management plan. This could include investors, employees, customers, or other key stakeholders.

| 6 |

Mindset Models

The *'do → have → be'* Mindset

The 'do-have-be' mindset is a way of thinking that focuses on external factors and actions. This mindset often involves the belief that your worth or value is determined by what you do or have. Your actions and possessions are seen as the most important determinants of your identity and worth. If you're caught up in this framework, you will need a regular reward. If you're programmed to get a salary every fortnight, it might be difficult to break the mould, as it may be a while before you see your first substantial cheque – and that's only if you succeed. The entrepreneurial journey may not be best suited for you unless you break this mindset. As the focus is inwards, and centred around the self, this mindset makes it difficult to focus on customer benefit centric approach.

The 'do-have-be' mindset can be motivating and great if you want to constantly achieve goals, but it can eventually lead to feelings of inadequacy if you don't achieve at par with or better than your previous accomplishments or what others are achieving. Someone wise has said that comparison is one of the easiest ways to destroy your happiness (expectations being another).

The '*be* → *do* → *have*' Mindset

The 'be-do-have' mindset, on the other hand, focuses on your internal factors and self-awareness. This mindset emphasises personal growth and development and encourages you to focus on your own values and beliefs. In this mindset, your worth isn't tied to what you do or have, but rather to who you are as a person. This simply signals that you're already where you need to be and just must do the work to create the outcome you desire. Your self-worth won't be entangled with the outcome you produce. Once you are in this state of mind, it is much easier to focus on providing benefits to your customer. You already feel adequate and are not trying to compete with your customers to ensure you keep the lion's share of benefit.

The 'be-do-have' mindset can promote self-acceptance and personal growth, but it can also lead to a lack of motivation if you don't feel a sense of purpose or direction. The best mindset will depend on you and your unique goals and needs. Intellectually, it's very easy to understand, but living it is difficult. Many successful people roam with imposter syndrome, while the imposters ooze with confidence and become hard to spot. This is simply because they have not given themselves permission to be where they are.

The 'be-do-have' mindset is what you need in your startup life and beyond, in general. Since creation first happens in your mind before it happens in the real world, you must be what you're aiming to be from the onset. It's difficult, so you need someone to coach or mentor you, someone to believe in you before you believe in yourself. You can't stop setbacks and challenges from happening, but if you live a life as if you're already at your destination, your mental agony of proving your self-worth associated with your venture's success will diminish. This way, you can focus objectively on the goals and benefits you are offering to others, without needing to prove anything to anyone else or worry about satisfying your own ego.

In the 'be-do-have' mindset, your worth is based on who you are as a person. You give yourself permission to achieve your goals without having the urge for seeking external validation. The 'be-do-have' mindset is a more positive and productive way of thinking that can help you in a startup setting to stay motivated, focused, and committed to achieving your goals.

Mindset Gives the Ability to Deal with Problems

Some of us are born into more advantageous circumstances, possessing wealth, privilege, or natural abilities, which makes it easier to succeed. It is also important to recognise that we can shape our own lives and circumstances through our actions, choices, and mindset, regardless of our starting point.

I know many amongst us have faced a series of unfortunate events, such as poverty, abuse, or discrimination, and lacked the resources, support, or opportunities that others may have had. Though it may seem that some were born into wealth, they may have had to overcome their fair share of challenges to achieve success. One common trait I have found among these individuals, was complete clarity of who they are and what they will do in life. It was never to do with possession, but always about the path they wanted to take and what they wanted to achieve—a clear, positive mindset.

Carol Dweck's concept of an "abundant mindset" refers to the belief that one's abilities, resources, and opportunities are not fixed, but rather can be expanded and developed over time. This mindset can be especially helpful for individuals who have faced significant challenges or adversity, as it helps them focus on their own potential and growth rather than their limitations.

I am reminded of the story of J.K. Rowling, the author of the Harry Potter series. Rowling faced significant challenges in her life, including poverty, depression, and the loss of her mother. Despite this, she achieved great success. Perhaps we can attribute it to her hard work, determination, and belief in her own abilities.

Your NPV or Net Present Value (as Human Capital)

When you immerse yourself in the pursuit of knowledge and consistently apply what you've learned, you elevate your own prospects and enhance the world around you in the present circumstances. By nurturing your human capital, which comprises the wisdom, skills, and abilities acquired through education, training, and experience, you raise your potential to generate income and contribute meaningfully to society.

Renowned economists often gauge an individual's human capital by considering the concept of net present value (NPV). This calculation, which discerns the worth of an investment in today's currency, takes into account the anticipated future income and tempers it with the time-value of money.

In the terms of human capital, one's NPV ascends when they are steadfast in their quest for knowledge and persistently strive to hone their skills. As you forge ahead, the world unfurls opportunities for you to generate income and contribute to the common good in the days to come. Just by being focussed and benefit oriented, you are enhancing the value of your offer to the world in future. That, in 'NPV terms', is enhancing your immediate value. You may realise it or not, but you are raising yourself and everyone around you.

By investing in your education and training, you lay the foundation for a prosperous future. The more you nurture your intellect and actively apply your knowledge and skills in your professional life, the greater your chances of reaping the rewards of your efforts and creating lasting value for yourself and others. This cultivates a higher NPV for your human capital compared to those who remain passive in their personal and professional growth. You are improving your future and present at the same time.

For the Reluctant Decision Makers Amongst Us

"More is lost by indecision than wrong decision. Indecision is the thief of opportunity. It will steal you blind." - Marcus Tullius Cicero

To elevate the quality of your life and achieve better outcomes in business or personal ventures, it's crucial to make decisions, even if they may not be perfect or ideal. As a founder you will be making critical decisions regularly. Some of them can make or break your business. When your decision can impact hundreds or thousands, it puts an immense pressure on the founder.

Decision-making can be daunting, and it's natural to feel uncertainty or hesitation when faced with choices. Avoiding decisions can often lead to negative consequences, such as missed opportunities, regret, or even paralysis.

Making a decision, even if it's not the 'right' one, can lead to valuable lessons and experiences. It can also help you gain confidence and become more decisive in the future. So, as you read this, remind yourself of the importance of taking action and making decisions, even in the face of uncertainty.

Once you train your decision-making muscle it will help you change your decisions rapidly in case you made a mistake. Good founders are not necessarily good decision makers, but they have an innate ability to decide and take necessary steps to amend their decisions.

Being in the Zone

Experiencing the state of being 'in the zone' for decision-making is an exceptional mental space where you're entirely absorbed, enabling you to make swift and effective decisions. The more decisions you make, the greater the chances that many of them will turn out to be sound choices. This cycle of successful decision-making paves the way for positive reinforcement and a self-fulfilling prophecy.

As you continue to make good decisions, the resultant positive outcomes will further fuel your motivation and enhance your ability to make even better decisions in the future. In this state of flow, you harness the power of your own intuition and expertise, propelling you towards even greater successes. Embrace this mindset, and you'll find yourself on an ever-ascending path of growth and achievement.

| 7 |

Not Everyone and Everything Is Competition

Repositioning and focusing on benefits also will move you away from how you perceive your competition.

Understanding Unique Business Journeys in Startups

In the competitive world of startups, the initial focus often gravitates towards competing with industry peers. This drive can sometimes lead to mimicking successful product features or services, a strategy aimed at capturing a share of the established market. However, it's crucial for startups to ensure that their offerings align with their target market's needs and resonate with their core values and objectives. This is your niche.

The Pitfalls of Comparisons

Drawing comparisons with competitors or industry benchmarks, while common, can lead to a skewed perception of one's unique journey. Each startup has its distinct set of experiences, challenges, and opportunities.

Comparing one's progress with others can foster feelings of inadequacy or unnecessary pressure, diverting focus from the startup's unique path and goals. Emphasising individual progress and aligning with one's own values is more productive than fitting into a preconceived mould or chasing after external expectations.

PayPal's Strategic Pivot

A notable example of a startup carving its unique path is PayPal in the late 1990s. Initially, PayPal positioned itself to compete with Billpoint, eBay's preferred online payment system. However, PayPal soon recognised that their primary users were eBay's customer base. Instead of direct competition, they pivoted to offer a more integrated, user-friendly payment solution for eBay users. This strategic shift not only differentiated PayPal from Billpoint but also led to its dominance in the online payment market and eventual acquisition by eBay in 2002.

Points to Ponder

PayPal's journey underscores the importance of understanding and adapting to market needs, rather than merely competing with existing solutions. For startups, this implies:

1. Identifying Unique Market Needs: understanding the unique needs of your target audience can reveal opportunities to innovate or improve upon existing solutions.

2. Aligning with Core Values: startups should ensure their product or service offerings align with their fundamental goals and values.

3. Embracing a Unique Path: each startup's journey is unique. Embracing this uniqueness can lead to innovative approaches and solutions that set a startup apart in the market.

| 8 |

Benefit-Focus Lets You Print Your Own Currency

In today's startup ecosystem, 'printing your own currency' symbolises a strategic approach where startups create unique value systems, such as followers, points, or even intangible aspects like a sense of happiness or security. This creative concept plays a pivotal role in how startups can leverage non-monetary facets to add benefits to their business model. It involves incentivising and engaging customers in non-traditional ways, turning these unique 'currencies' into tangible assets for the company. This approach is integral for startups seeking innovative ways to build customer relationships, drive engagement, and foster a sense of community around their products or services. Understanding and effectively implementing this strategy can lead to sustainable growth, as it opens new avenues for customer interaction and value creation, transcending conventional monetary transactions. In this section we are discussing some intangible benefits. They can end up making your customers feel happy or satisfy your ego or even have a potential of higher profits.

Likes

Though this benefit is intangible, often people have risked their lives doing dangerous stunts just to collect more likes in social media. In the dynamic social media landscape, 'likes' have evolved into a nuanced form of currency, significantly impacting the digital economy across platforms like Facebook, Instagram, and TikTok. Each 'like' on these platforms does more than express user approval; it actively influences content algorithms, determining visibility, reach, and engagement.

On Facebook, likes are a crucial metric in gauging the popularity and reach of posts, pages, and ads. They signal to Facebook's algorithms that the content is valuable and worthy of higher ranking and visibility in users' news feeds. This enhanced exposure can lead to a chain reaction of increased interaction - more likes, comments, shares, and crucially, clicks. These interactions are vital, especially for businesses and advertisers on the platform, as they translate into direct revenue generation through targeted advertising and increased consumer engagement.

Similarly, on Instagram, likes serve as a barometer of content engagement and popularity, shaping the reach and influence of posts and profiles. They play a critical role in dictating the content's visibility on users' feeds and the Explore page, directly impacting the success of influencer marketing and commercial campaigns. High engagement rates, signalled by a large number of likes, are often sought after by brands for partnerships, as they indicate a high level of audience interaction and influence.

TikTok, a platform driven by trends and virality, also leverages likes as a fundamental engagement metric. Here, likes not only signify audience approval but also contribute to the virality potential of a video. TikTok's algorithm considers likes as a key factor in determining what content gets featured more prominently on users' 'For You' pages. The cascading effect of likes on TikTok can catapult content to viral status, making it a coveted metric for creators and marketers aiming to capture widespread attention rapidly.

The economic implications of likes on these platforms are profound. They have given rise to a thriving industry of digital marketing and influencer engagement, where likes are often directly correlated with monetisation opportunities and brand partnerships. For businesses and creators, understanding the nuances of these engagement metrics and harnessing their potential is crucial for digital strategy success. Likes have transcended their original purpose as mere indicators of preference, becoming key drivers in the complex algorithms that govern content dissemination and success in the digital realm.

The likes in the social media ecosystem serve as more than digital nods of approval; they are instrumental in content strategy, digital marketing, and, ultimately, the monetisation of online presence. They underscore the transition of social media from platforms of mere social interaction to powerful engines driving the digital economy.

Followers

On Platform X and across other social media platforms like Instagram and TikTok, followers have transformed from a mere count of social connections into a monetisable asset. Instagram, for example, leverages followers as a metric of influence, crucial for influencer marketing and targeted advertisements. TikTok, on the other hand, uses follower dynamics to drive content virality and brand partnerships. This paradigm shift in the valuation of followers highlights the intricate relationship between social metrics and the digital economy. It's a nuanced ecosystem where follower counts reflect popularity and translate into potential revenue streams through advertising, sponsorships, and influencer collaborations. The strategic use of followers by these platforms demonstrates an understanding of their multifaceted value – as indicators of reach, influencers of algorithmic content dissemination, and drivers of engagement and profitability.

Stars

Star ratings have become a critical element in the ecosystem of numerous online platforms, extending beyond ride-sharing apps like Uber to include a wide array of services and products. These platforms range from e-commerce giants like Amazon and eBay to hospitality services like Airbnb, and even extend to app stores for mobile devices. The ubiquitous nature of star ratings across these diverse platforms underscores their significance as a measure of quality, customer satisfaction, and popularity.

In Uber, for example, the star rating system is intricately linked to the service experience, influencing the visibility and match quality of both riders and drivers. High ratings can enhance user experiences, leading to a cycle where improved ratings correlate with better service and higher earnings. This dynamic has given rise to an ancillary market where users actively seek ways to enhance their ratings, recognising their monetary value in the platform's ecosystem.

The monetisation of star ratings reflects a broader trend in digital platforms where user-generated feedback becomes a valuable commodity. It's a phenomenon that Sangeet Paul Choudhary[3] explores in depth in his works, shedding light on the intricate dynamics of digital platform economies. His insights delve into how such mechanisms not only drive user engagement but also shape the economic model of digital platforms.

Platform Stickiness

Followers, likes and stars make the platform sticky. If you are a builder of a platform your customers are more likely to stay on your platform if they are good as they have followers likes or stars. Should they move on to other platforms offering similar services, they have to start from scratch. You have the first mover advantage. That said, your good customers with high rating and interaction will continue to use your platform and the ones that are not rated well enough will have a greater incentive to jump platform. This is useful for virality in growth as well.

Brand

Numerous luxury brands have elevated their stature and allure to such an extent that consumers are not only willing to pay premium prices but also resort to the black market to acquire their products. This phenomenon is a testament to the immense prestige and exclusivity these brands symbolise. The value and reputation of their offerings are not merely intrinsic but also appreciative over time, making them coveted assets in the eyes of many.

Brands like Hermès, Louis Vuitton, and Rolex are exemplary in this regard. They are synonymous with exceptional quality, meticulous craftsmanship, and a sense of exclusivity. These attributes have cemented their positions as symbols of luxury, prestige, and status. Consequently, their products command high prices, often driving enthusiasts to the black market in search of these luxury items.

Take, for instance, the Hermès Birkin bag. Renowned for its craftsmanship and rarity, it can command prices upwards of tens of thousands of dollars. The allure and demand are so high that it's not uncommon to find these bags fetching even higher prices on the black market. Similarly, Louis Vuitton handbags, celebrated for their iconic designs and quality, can reach thousands of dollars in retail and even more in underground markets. Rolex watches, with their timeless design and precision engineering, are also sought after in the black market, sometimes fetching prices well into the tens of thousands. The details of brand building are beyond the current scope of this book.

Safety

Fear not, the help is near. In the world of startups, I have found an increasing trend of creating a unique form of currency that capitalises on the human desire for safety and security. This conceptual currency transcends traditional monetary value, instead offering a sense of safety as its primary commodity. This approach transcends across various domains, from tangible products to digital solutions.

1. Consumer Goods as Safety Currency: in this case, startups are redefining everyday consumer goods – like home security devices, personal alarms, and self-defence tools – as more than just products. They are marketed as tokens of safety, each purchase acting like an investment in personal security. While the physical effectiveness of these items can vary, their value as a currency lies in the psychological assurance they provide, embodying a tangible symbol of safety in the hands of the consumer.

2. Digital Platforms Offering Perceived Safety: digital services and apps, such as emergency response apps, location-tracking systems, and VPNs, are being positioned by startups as a digital currency of safety. These platforms offer basic protection in their free versions, but their premium services are marketed as a higher denomination in the safety currency, promising enhanced security features. While the actual increase in safety might be subjective, the perceived value in these digital offerings is what these startups are banking on – selling peace of mind as a service.

3. Professional Services as Personalised Safety Assurance: startups are also venturing into professional services like personal security, private investigation, and bodyguard services, treating them as high-value safety currency. These services offer direct and personalised safety solutions, often carrying a higher perceived value due to their tailored and active approach to security. The

effectiveness of these services is more pronounced, but their role as a part of this unique safety currency ecosystem is to provide an elite level of comfort and assurance.

By creating this new currency of safety, startups are not just selling products or services; they are trading in the currency of tranquillity and assurance. This innovative approach encourages customers to view safety not just as a necessity, but as a valuable asset that can be acquired, enhanced, and traded. It's a paradigm shift that challenges traditional notions of value, placing safety and peace of mind at the forefront of consumer priorities.

Happiness

The monetisation of happiness in consumer culture extends across various sectors, transforming the idea of happiness from an intangible emotional state into a tangible asset. Luxury consumer goods like high-end vacations, gourmet foods, and designer fashion are marketed as more than mere products; they're sold as experiences or gateways to happiness. This marketing strategy, leveraging the allure of an enhanced lifestyle, justifies the premium prices these products command. You want to boost your ego? The sky's the limit.

In the digital world, apps focusing on meditation, wellness, and fitness, as well as social media platforms, harness a similar concept. They offer basic services for free but promote premium features promising greater happiness, thus tapping into the user's pursuit of emotional well-being. This freemium model cleverly balances accessibility with the lure of an upgraded experience.

The self-help and personal development industry capitalises on this trend by offering books, courses, and seminars that promise pathways to happiness and personal growth. Unlike tangible luxury goods, these products sell the promise of intangible self-improvement, often at substantial costs.

This widespread commodification of happiness reflects a deep understanding of modern consumer psychology. It highlights a shift in marketing strategies - from selling products and services based on their functional value to selling them as means of achieving emotional satisfaction. This shift indicates a broader societal trend where emotional well-being is increasingly valued and sought after, making happiness a lucrative commodity in the marketplace. First you tell the problem then you provide steps to solve it.

The strategy of monetising happiness across these sectors showcases the evolving relationship between consumerism, marketing, and the universal human pursuit of happiness. It underscores how modern marketing transcends traditional approaches, embedding emotional value into products and services.

Time

The concept of 'time' as a currency in the modern market is gaining traction, with numerous products and services claiming to save customers' valuable time. This includes a wide array of offerings, from meal delivery services and home cleaning robots to productivity apps and online shopping platforms. These innovations are designed to streamline everyday tasks, allowing consumers to allocate their time more effectively. In a world where time is increasingly precious, these products and services are not just selling convenience; they're selling the promise of more time - a commodity that many consider invaluable. This trend reflects a shift in consumer priorities, where saving time is often as valuable as saving money.

Consumer Goods and Services: Enhancing Time Efficiency

Consumer goods and services, such as advanced home appliances, cleaning and maintenance services, and meal delivery options, are strategically designed to save consumers' time. These products, often carrying a higher price tag, are not just selling functionality but are marketed as solutions to optimise daily efficiency and productivity. The value proposition of these offerings is clear: by reducing the time spent on mundane tasks, they allow consumers to focus on more meaningful activities, thus enhancing their overall quality of life.

Digital Services and Apps: Streamlining Daily Operations

The digital realm, with its array of productivity and time-management apps, scheduling tools, and online shopping services, is a testament to the value of time in the modern age. These platforms, offering both free and premium versions, are engineered to simplify and accelerate everyday tasks. From automating routine processes to facilitating quick decision-making, these digital tools are invaluable for saving time, often translating into improved productivity and efficiency for their users.

Professional Services: Offering Expert Time-Saving Solutions

In the sphere of professional services, offerings like personal assistant services, concierge services, and virtual assistants stand out. These services, typically commanding a higher price, are marketed on the promise of saving time. They provide expert assistance, manage day-to-day tasks, and offer support in decision-making processes. For consumers who value their time highly, these services become an essential investment, enabling them to delegate routine tasks and focus on more strategic or enjoyable activities.

| 9 |

Customer Benefit: The Endgame of Your Decisions

"Take a simple basic idea and take it very seriously." - Charlie Munger

Your purpose for being in business is to create and appropriate value. These two components may not be in direct correlation. Often many entrepreneurs tend to skew this in their favour and appropriate more than they create. There is arbitrage in the cost of value creation and value appropriation. The greater the arbitrage, the more profitable the venture. A successful business endeavours to generate value by offering benefit to its customers in a sustaining way. An elaborate list is being shared here which will help you in creating a strategy canvas[2] when you compare your business with your competition. Following this is a repertoire of these benefits. You will find that successful companies are formed by simply being exceptional at a single benefit. This list should be a reference only, as you may be able to create your own benchmarks.

Functional Benefits

These are the tangible, practical benefits that a product or service provides. For example, a customer may be willing to pay for a car because it provides transportation, or for a lawnmower because it helps them to maintain their yard. Different types of functional benefits include:

Ease of Use

Your offer of a product or service can be enhanced if it is easy to use, which saves customers both time and effort.

Trello, a cloud-based project management tool, focuses on ease of use with its visually appealing board system. Users can effortlessly create, assign, and organise tasks as cards, while labels, checklists, and due dates. Real-time updates and simple communication enable seamless team collaboration, making Trello an intuitive choice for managing projects.

Dropbox, a cloud storage service, emphasises ease of use by allowing users to effortlessly sync and share files across multiple devices. Its clean interface and drag-and-drop features make file management intuitive. With seamless integration into various platforms, Dropbox simplifies collaboration and file accessibility, making it an appealing choice for users seeking straightforward file storage solutions.

Wix, a website builder, prioritises ease of use with its drag-and-drop editor, enabling users to create professional-looking websites without coding skills. With a variety of templates and design elements, Wix makes website creation accessible to anyone. Its intuitive interface and guided process ensure that users can quickly and easily build a visually appealing online presence, catering to those who prefer a user-friendly website building experience.

Look at your product or service. How can you make it easier to use? Focus on creating a seamless user experience that saves time and effort for your customers. Instead of walking five minutes, people normalise ordering via Uber from a shop just across the road... and pay extra. What I discovered about this from a business owner is that "people are lazy, busy or just want it easy." This is a business model that works.

Quality

You might offer a high-quality product or service that is built to last and performs well. A startup that manufactures high-quality outdoor gear might offer products that are durable and can withstand harsh conditions, providing customers with long-lasting value.

Leica Camera AG stands out in the photography industry for its exceptionally high-quality cameras and lenses, renowned for their unparalleled image quality, build, and performance.

Vitamix has built its reputation on the exceptional quality of its high-performance blenders, offering a superior blending experience through their powerful motors and durable construction.

What would it take for your customers to see your product as the gold standard? For example, Pari Rice has maintained a standard for Premium Basmati Rice in Dubai and buyers compare other rice brands with it... "is it as good as Pari" is often used. Likewise, Dilmah Tea from Sri Lanka has maintained a gold standard benchmark. Both are simple products, perhaps every step in the process has been perfected by these businesses.

Efficiency

You might offer a product or service that helps customers work more efficiently, by automating tasks or streamlining processes.

A startup that provides an AI-powered customer service platform might help businesses automate routine tasks, freeing up time for more complex and valuable work.

Zoom gained significant popularity due to its efficient and reliable video conferencing platform, providing users with a seamless virtual meeting experience even during periods of high demand.

The Swedish furniture company IKEA is known for its efficient flat-pack furniture design and streamlined self-assembly process, allowing customers to save on shipping costs and easily transport their purchases home.

Cost Savings

You might offer a product or service that helps customers save money, either by reducing their operating costs or by providing a more affordable alternative to existing solutions.

TransferWise (now Wise) is a money transfer service that provides customers with a cost-effective way to send money internationally by using a peer-to-peer system to reduce fees and offer more favourable exchange rates compared to traditional banks.

Giffgaff is a UK-based mobile virtual network operator (MVNO) that offers SIM-only plans and pay-as-you-go options, with low-cost plans and no contracts. Their unique community-driven approach to customer support helps them keep operational costs low, passing the savings onto customers.

Customisation

Your startup might offer a product or service that can be customised to meet the specific needs of each customer.

Vistaprint is an online printing company that allows customers to create custom marketing materials such as business cards, banners, and promotional products. Vistaprint offers a wide range of templates and design options, enabling customers to personalise their items to suit their specific needs and preferences.

Function of Beauty is a hair care company that exists solely to provide fully customised shampoo and conditioner based on customers' unique hair type, hair goals, and preferences. Customers take a quiz to determine their specific hair needs and can even customise the colour, fragrance, and name of their products. Function of Beauty's entire business model is built on providing personalised haircare solutions to cater to individual hair care needs.

Reliability

You might offer a product or service that is reliable and consistently performs as expected.

Backblaze is an online backup service that offers customers reliable, continuous data protection by securely backing up their files to the cloud. Known for its ease of use and dependable backup system, Backblaze provides peace of mind to users that their data is safe.

Moleskine is a brand known for its high-quality notebooks, journals, and planners; Moleskine has built a reputation for reliability in the stationery industry. With durable covers, acid-free paper, and a variety of formats, customers trust Moleskine products for their consistent performance and long-lasting quality.

Versatility

You might offer a product or service that can be used in a variety of different situations or environments.

Leatherman, a company that specialises in multi-tools, has built its brand around the concept of versatility. Their innovative products combine various tools, such as pliers, knives, screwdrivers, and more, into a single, compact device that can be easily carried and used for various tasks, making them a favourite among outdoor enthusiasts and DIYers.

GoPro is known for its versatile action cameras that cater to adventure enthusiasts, content creators, and casual users alike. These compact cameras offer high-quality video and photo capabilities, with a range of accessories and mounting options that allow users to capture content in various scenarios, such as underwater, while biking, or during extreme sports. The flexibility and adaptability of GoPro cameras have made them a popular choice for capturing unique and dynamic content.

Safety

As a startup you might offer a product or service that is designed with safety in mind, helping to protect customers and their assets.

As an example, Britax is a global manufacturer of child car seats, strollers, and travel systems and is known for its dedication to child safety. Their car seats consistently receive top ratings for safety and ease of use, with a focus on innovative design, rigorous testing, and attention to detail. Britax's commitment to child safety has made them a trusted choice for parents seeking reliable and secure products for their children.

Another example, Bluebell is a startup that has developed an innovative baby monitor system designed to ensure the safety and well-being of babies. The system includes a wearable monitor for the baby, a parent wristband, and a smart hub. The baby monitor tracks the baby's breathing, skin temperature, sleep position, and movement, alerting parents if anything is out of the ordinary. The focus on safety and peace of mind for parents has made Bluebell a popular choice in the baby monitor market.

Convenience

As a startup founder, your aim could be to provide a product or service that focuses on offering maximum convenience to your users. By ensuring easy accessibility and availability, you cater to their needs for simplicity and flexibility. You should aim to provide a user experience that prioritises convenience, making your customers' lives easier and hassle-free.

Airtasker is an Australian platform connecting users with local freelancers to help them complete various tasks and chores, such as handyman work, cleaning, gardening, and moving assistance. Users can post their tasks, browse available workers based on skills and reviews, and pay securely through the app. Airtasker offers a convenient way for Australians to get everyday tasks done by reliable professionals with ease.

Blinkist is a mobile app offering summaries of non-fiction books, allowing users to absorb key insights from popular titles in just 15 minutes. With a vast library of book summaries, users can gain knowledge and discover new interests quickly and conveniently.

Innovation

As a founder, your startup might offer a product or service that is innovative, utilising new technologies or approaches to solve problems in novel ways. By focusing on innovation, you can provide unique value to your customers, differentiate yourself from competitors, and create a strong brand identity.

Beyond Meat has created a range of plant-based meat alternatives that taste and feel like traditional meat. Their innovative approach to using plant proteins have made them a leader in the market and has attracted many consumers looking for sustainable and healthier options.

Echogen developed a waste heat-to-power solution that turns excess heat from industrial processes into clean electricity. Their innovative technology increases energy efficiency, reduces emissions, and offers a cost-effective way for industries to generate additional power, revolutionising waste-heat management.

Emotional Benefits

As a startup founder, it's important to recognise the emotional benefits your product or service can provide to your customers. These benefits can create strong connections, driving customer loyalty and satisfaction. Emphasise on addressing customer pain points and delivering positive experiences that resonate with them emotionally.

Happiness

As a startup founder, focus on developing products or services that bring happiness and joy to your customers. Offering a sense of fun or fulfillment that meets their needs, generates positive emotions, and creates memorable experiences. This could involve providing unique entertainment options or designing thoughtful, personalised products that bring delight to both the giver and the receiver.

The Adventure Junkies is a startup that focuses on creating memorable experiences for outdoor enthusiasts by offering curated adventure trips. They bring happiness to their customers by helping them connect with nature, learn new skills, and create lasting memories.

The Sill is a startup that specialises in indoor plants, offering a wide variety of houseplants, planters, and accessories. Their mission is to make the experience of discovering the perfect potted plants for your environment as enjoyable as possible, bringing happiness to customers by enhancing their living spaces with beautiful, air-purifying greenery.

Pride

As a startup founder, it's important to understand how your product or service can instil a sense of pride in your customers. By aligning with their values or contributing to a cause they care about, you can create a strong emotional connection that drives customer loyalty and satisfaction. Focus on developing offerings that empower customers to make choices they can be proud of, whether it's through sustainable practices, ethical sourcing, or promoting social causes.

Patagonia, founded by Yvon Chouinard, is an outdoor clothing and gear company renowned for its commitment to environmental and social responsibility. The Chouinard family transferred their $3 billion ownership of Patagonia to a trust and a non-profit organisation, ensuring that all profits — about $100 million a year — are used to combat climate change and protect undeveloped land around the globe. Customers take pride in supporting a brand that shares their values and actively works towards a positive impact with its unconventional spin on capitalism.

TOMS shoe company is dedicated to improving lives through its business model. When customers buy TOMS products, they help fund access to mental health resources for millions of people who need them. By investing one-third of its profits for grassroots good, TOMS supports community organisations and drives sustainable change. Customers feel proud to be part of a movement that directly contributes to making the world a better place through their purchasing decisions.

Security

As a startup founder, understanding the security benefits your product or service provides to customers is crucial. By ensuring safety and protection, you build trust and confidence in your brand. Focus on developing solutions that guard against potential risks, promote financial stability, or instil a sense of well-being, as this will resonate with customers who value security and peace of mind.

Proton Mail is a Swiss-based startup that offers a secure and encrypted email service, ensuring the privacy and security of its users' communications. By using end-to-end encryption and hosting their servers in privacy-friendly jurisdictions, Proton Mail enables customers to communicate safely without the worry of their messages being intercepted or read by unauthorised parties.

Haven Life is a US-based startup that offers an innovative online platform for purchasing term life insurance policies. By streamlining the application process and providing transparent pricing, Haven Life enables customers to secure their financial future and protect their loved ones with ease and confidence.

Self-esteem

As a startup founder, you might consider developing a product or service that enhances customers' self-esteem by catering to their personal growth or aspirations. By creating solutions that support their journey towards self-improvement or provide a sense of achievement, you enable customers to feel more confident and positive about themselves. This could involve offering customised solutions, fostering skill development, or facilitating personal transformation.

Rent the Runway is a fashion rental platform that provides customers access to designer clothing and accessories for a fraction of the retail cost. By allowing customers to wear high-quality, fashionable clothing for special occasions or everyday life, Rent the Runway helps boost self-esteem by making users feel more confident and stylish in their appearance.

MasterClass is an online learning platform that offers courses taught by world-renowned experts in various fields, such as cooking, filmmaking, writing, and more. By providing users with access to high-quality education and the opportunity to develop new skills, MasterClass helps boost self-esteem as users gain confidence in their abilities and feel a sense of accomplishment.

Self-expression

A startup might offer a product or service that enables customers to express themselves creatively, showcasing their individuality and unique perspective. By providing a platform for self-expression, the startup empowers users to feel more connected to themselves, and to others who share similar interests or passions. This fosters a sense of belonging and community, while also promoting personal growth and self-discovery.

Etsy is an online marketplace that allows artisans and crafters to sell their unique, handmade, and vintage products. This platform enables creative individuals to express themselves through their work and connect with customers who appreciate and value their one-of-a-kind creations.

Redbubble is an online platform where independent artists can showcase and sell their artwork on a variety of products such as clothing, home decor, and accessories. This allows artists to express themselves and reach a broader audience, while customers can discover and purchase unique items that resonate with their own sense of style and self-expression.

Belonging

A startup might offer a product or service that helps customers feel connected to others by creating a sense of community or fostering relationships. This sense of belonging can be a powerful driver for customer loyalty and satisfaction, as people naturally seek connections and shared experiences.

Meetup is an online platform that allows users to create and join groups based on their interests, hobbies, or professional pursuits. By hosting events and facilitating in-person or virtual gatherings, Meetup helps people find and connect with others who share their passions, creating a sense of belonging and community.

Peloton is a fitness company that offers at-home workout equipment and classes through a subscription service. With a strong focus on community and connection, Peloton allows users to join live classes, compete with friends, and engage with instructors and other members. This sense of belonging and support helps motivate users and contributes to the overall success of the platform.

Comfort

Startups might offer a product or service that delivers physical or emotional comfort, contributing to stress relief or enhancing the quality of life for customers. By addressing customers' needs for relaxation and self-care, such a startup can create positive experiences, fostering customer loyalty and satisfaction.

Calm is a popular meditation and sleep app designed to help users reduce stress, improve sleep, and promote overall well-being. Through guided meditations, sleep stories, and calming music, Calm provides emotional comfort and relaxation, helping users manage stress and anxiety.

Gravity Blankets offers high-quality weighted blankets designed to promote relaxation and improve sleep. By simulating the sensation of a comforting hug, weighted blankets help users feel physically and emotionally comforted, leading to reduced stress and better sleep quality. It is known as an anxiety solution.

Escape

A startup might offer a product or service that enables customers to transcend the mundane aspects of daily life, presenting them with opportunities for rejuvenation and exploration. By creating innovative and immersive experiences, these startups transport customers to new realms or mindsets, allowing them to rediscover their sense of wonder and curiosity.

Meow Wolf is an immersive art collective that designs and constructs unique, interactive exhibits and installations. With their visually captivating and hands-on experiences, Meow Wolf offers visitors a chance to escape into otherworldly environments, stimulating their creativity and imagination.

The Secret Cinema is a London-based company that creates immersive cinematic experiences, where viewers become part of the story. By combining film, theatre, and live action, The Secret Cinema transports participants to the world of their favourite movies, offering a one-of-a-kind escape from everyday life and a deeper connection to the stories they love.

Control

A startup might offer a product or service that empowers customers to regain command over their lives or circumstances, by delivering innovative solutions and resources for efficient decision-making and task management. Equipping individuals with the means to navigate their personal or professional domains, these startups foster confidence and self-efficacy.

RescueTime is a time management software that helps users understand and optimise how they spend their time on digital devices. Helping track computer and smartphone usage, categorising activities, and providing productivity reports, RescueTime enables individuals to take control of their daily routines and make conscious choices for better time management and work-life balance.

Up Bank is an Australian digital bank that provides a mobile-first banking experience, helping users take control of their finances. Up Bank's app enables customers to easily track spending, categorise transactions, set saving goals, and receive real-time insights into their financial habits.

Empowerment

A startup might offer a product or service that enables customers to feel empowered by equipping them with the necessary skills, knowledge, and resources to thrive in their personal or professional lives. A startup that offers comprehensive training programs, mentorship, or educational resources can help customers develop their abilities, unlock their potential, and ultimately, feel more in control of their own success.

General Assembly is a global educational company that offers in-person and online courses in various fields such as web development, data science, and digital marketing. By providing practical, skill-based education, the General Assembly empowers individuals to succeed in today's competitive job market and reach their career goals.

Skillshare is an online learning community offering thousands of creative, business, and technology classes. By providing a wide range of accessible courses, Skillshare empowers individuals to develop new skills, explore their passions, and enhance their personal or professional growth.

Social Benefits

A startup focused on offering social benefits strives to boost customers' social standing, acceptance, and belonging within their communities. By supplying products or services that represent prestige, exclusivity, or adherence to cultural norms, these startups help customers enhance their social position and forge meaningful connections. Genuine, socially driven startups can create a lasting and positive impact on society by nurturing authentic connections and promoting values that resonate with their audience. The true spirit of such a startup lies in its ability to genuinely contribute to society's improvement and enrich the lives of its customers.

Community Building

A startup centred on community building offers products or services that cultivate connections and a sense of belonging among individuals. By fostering supportive networks and shared experiences, these startups enrich their customers' lives and contribute to a more cohesive society.

Couchsurfing connects travellers with locals who offer a place to stay or meet up, promoting cultural exchange and friendship among its global community. It encourages users to share experiences, learn from each other, and form lasting connections.

Nextdoor is a private social networking app designed to connect neighbours and foster a sense of community within local areas. Users can share local news, recommendations, events, and classifieds, as well as organise neighbourhood activities, ultimately strengthening bonds within the community.

Environmental Sustainability

A startup focused on environmental stability develops products or services that contribute to the preservation and protection of the planet's ecosystems. By promoting sustainable practices, reducing waste, or conserving resources, these startups pave the way for a healthier environment and a more sustainable future. Often, all being equal, this becomes a deciding factor when making a purchase decision.

Ecolife Recycling is dedicated to creating innovative recycling solutions for a wide range of materials, including plastics, metals, and electronics. By transforming waste into valuable resources, Ecolife supports a circular economy, reducing pollution and preserving the environment for future generations.

Ecovative Design specialises in creating sustainable alternatives to traditional materials using mycelium, the root structure of mushrooms. Their eco-friendly products replace plastic, foam, and other materials with a biodegradable and renewable option, actively contributing to a more sustainable world.

Health and Wellness is a startup focused on health and wellness aims to improve the physical, mental, and emotional well-being of individuals through innovative products or services. By offering solutions that promote a healthy lifestyle, prevent illness, or support mental health, these startups contribute to the overall quality of life and the betterment of society.

Headspace is a popular meditation and mindfulness app that provides guided meditation sessions, mindfulness exercises, and sleep assistance. Its purpose is to help users reduce stress, improve focus, and enhance their mental well-being; Headspace supports a healthier, more balanced lifestyle.

Noom is a weight loss and health management app that combines personalised coaching, food tracking, and behavioural psychology to help users create sustainable, healthy habits. By offering tailored guidance and support, Noom empowers individuals to take control of their health and achieve lasting wellness.

Education

A startup focused on education aims to enhance learning and skill development through innovative products or services. By offering solutions that facilitate knowledge acquisition, skill improvement, and personal growth, these startups contribute to the intellectual advancement of individuals and the overall betterment of society.

Coursera is an online learning platform that partners with top universities and organisations worldwide, offering a broad range of courses, specialisations, and degree programs. By providing accessible, high-quality education across various subjects, Coursera empowers individuals to learn new skills, advance their careers, or explore personal interests.

Duolingo is a language learning app that offers interactive, gamified lessons in multiple languages. By making language learning engaging and accessible, Duolingo helps users improve their language skills, break down cultural barriers, and broaden their personal and professional opportunities.

Charitable Giving

A startup focused on charitable giving aims to facilitate and encourage philanthropy by providing innovative solutions that make it easier for individuals and organisations to donate or support social causes. These startups empower people to make a positive impact on society while promoting a culture of generosity and compassion.

GiveWell is an organisation that conducts in-depth research and analysis on charities to determine their effectiveness and impact. By providing donors with data-driven recommendations, GiveWell helps individuals make informed decisions about where to allocate their charitable donations, ensuring that their contributions create the most significant positive impact.

DonorsChoose is an online crowdfunding platform that connects public school teachers with donors who want to support educational projects. Teachers post project requests for materials or experiences their students need, and donors can contribute directly to those projects, enabling the teachers to enhance their students' learning experiences and opportunities.

Employment

A startup focused on employment aims to bridge the gap between job seekers and employers by offering innovative solutions and services that streamline the hiring process, match candidates with suitable job opportunities, and facilitate career growth. These startups contribute to a robust job market and help individuals find fulfilling employment that aligns with their skills and aspirations.

LinkedIn is a professional networking platform that connects job seekers, employers, and professionals across various industries. The platform allows users to create professional profiles, showcase their skills and achievements, discover job opportunities, and connect with potential employers. LinkedIn has become an essential tool for both job seekers and companies looking to hire top talent.

Indeed is a leading job search engine that aggregates job listings from various sources, including company websites, job boards, and staffing agencies. Users can search for job opportunities using keywords and location filters, upload their resumes, and apply for positions directly through the platform. Indeed also offers tools for employers to post job listings, manage applicants, and discover potential candidates.

Social Justice

A startup focused on social justice aims to address inequalities and injustices by offering products or services that promote fairness, inclusivity, and equal opportunities for all. These startups work to dismantle systemic barriers and empower marginalised communities through innovative solutions, advocacy, and education.

Color Of Change is a progressive non-profit civil rights advocacy organisation that focuses on fighting for racial justice and equality. They use online campaigns, grassroots organising, and strategic partnerships to create change in policies, practices, and public opinion. By mobilising their members, Colour Of Change amplifies the voices of marginalised communities and drives tangible social change.

Kiva is a non-profit organisation that facilitates microloans to underprivileged entrepreneurs and individuals in developing countries. Through their online platform, lenders can contribute as little as $25 to help fund small businesses, education, or other essential needs for borrowers. By providing access to capital and financial services, Kiva empowers individuals to break the cycle of poverty and create sustainable change in their communities.

Cultural Enrichment

A startup focused on cultural enrichment aims to promote the appreciation, understanding, and celebration of diverse cultures, arts, and traditions. These startups offer products or services that encourage people to engage with various cultures, fostering a sense of global citizenship, tolerance, and respect for cultural diversity.

Global Voices is a non-profit online community of volunteer writers, translators, and digital activists dedicated to amplifying underrepresented voices and perspectives from around the world. By publishing news stories, opinion pieces, and translations in multiple languages,

Global Voices encourages cross-cultural understanding, stimulates dialogue, and fosters a sense of global community. The platform serves as a valuable resource for cultural enrichment and a space for diverse voices to be heard.

Public Safety

A startup focused on public safety strives to create products or services that protect and enhance the well-being of communities, ensuring that individuals feel secure in their surroundings. These startups work towards reducing crime, accidents, and other threats to public safety, ultimately contributing to the development of safer, more resilient communities.

SoundThinking is a technology company that specialises in gunshot detection and location services. By using acoustic sensors and advanced algorithms, SoundThinking can quickly and accurately detect and locate gunfire incidents in real-time, allowing law enforcement and emergency responders to react more efficiently. This technology aids in reducing gun violence and improving overall public safety.

RapidSOS is an emergency technology startup that connects people, devices, and apps directly to 9-1-1 and first responders during emergencies. Their platform provides precise location data, medical information, and real-time situational awareness to emergency responders, helping to improve response times and save lives. RapidSOS is dedicated to enhancing public safety through innovative technology and collaboration with emergency services.

Quality of Life

A startup focused on improving quality of life aims to create products or services that enhance the overall well-being, happiness, and satisfaction of individuals and communities. These startups work towards addressing various aspects of life, such as health, comfort, convenience, and social connections, ultimately contributing to a more fulfilling and balanced lifestyle.

Blue Apron is a meal kit delivery service that aims to make home cooking more accessible, enjoyable, and sustainable. By providing pre-portioned ingredients and easy-to-follow recipes, Blue Apron helps users create delicious, healthy meals while reducing food waste and simplifying meal planning. The service promotes a better quality of life through the enjoyment of nutritious, home-cooked food and the convenience of a meal delivery service.

Personal Benefits

Personal benefits encompass the advantages that a product or service delivers in terms of individual growth, satisfaction, and well-being. These benefits cater to the unique needs and aspirations of each customer, enabling them to enhance their skills, knowledge, or overall sense of contentment. By investing in products or services that offer personal benefits, individuals can experience self-improvement, personal development, and the enrichment of their lives. Some themes for you to ponder and incorporate as needed. Please ensure you focus on a limited set of benefits from this large repertoire provided as some benefits might cannibalise the other.

Personal Development

Personal development focuses on helping individuals grow, learn, and improve various aspects of their lives. Startups that offer products or services aimed at personal development can empower customers to achieve their goals, enhance their skills, and become better versions of themselves.

BetterUp is an online coaching platform that connects users with certified coaches to help them improve various aspects of their personal and professional lives. BetterUp offers personalised coaching sessions in areas such as leadership, communication, work-life balance, and personal growth, empowering individuals to achieve their potential and overcome obstacles.

Comfort

A startup might offer a product or service that enhances comfort for its customers, by providing physical or emotional relief and improving their overall well-being. These startups focus on alleviating stress and creating a sense of ease in the lives of their users.

Yogibo is a company that creates innovative, comfortable furniture, such as bean bags, pillows, and body supports. Their products are designed to mould and conform to the user's body shape, providing personalised comfort and support. With a focus on relaxation and stress relief, Yogibo's products contribute to improving the quality of life for their customers.

Self-improvement

A startup might offer a product or service that focuses on self-improvement, providing customers with the tools, resources, or guidance needed to develop new skills, achieve personal goals, or enhance their overall well-being. These startups aim to empower individuals to become the best versions of themselves.

Skillshare is an online learning platform that offers thousands of classes across various categories, such as design, business, technology, and personal development. It provides access to a wide range of courses and expert instructors, Skillshare helps users build new skills and grow both personally and professionally.

Headspace is a mindfulness and meditation app that assists users in improving their mental well-being and overall life satisfaction. With guided meditation sessions, exercises focused on stress reduction, and sleep aids, Headspace empowers individuals to take control of their mental health and work on personal growth through mindfulness practices.

Convenience

As a startup founder you might offer a product or service that focuses on convenience, by simplifying daily tasks, streamlining processes, or saving your customers time and effort. By doing this you will aim to make life easier for your users by providing seamless and efficient solutions to common problems.

Instacart is an online grocery delivery service that allows customers to shop from local stores and have their groceries delivered to their doorsteps. By offering a user-friendly platform and efficient delivery service, Instacart provides convenience to busy individuals who may not have the time to do their grocery shopping in person.

TaskRabbit is a platform that connects people with local, skilled 'Taskers' who can help with various tasks, such as home repairs, furniture assembly, and moving assistance. (AirTasker works on a similar business model in Australia.) By providing a reliable and convenient way to find and book help for everyday tasks, TaskRabbit saves customers time and energy while ensuring that their needs are met.

Personalisation and Customisation

As a startup you might offer a product or service that focuses on customisation, allowing customers to 'tailor' their experience or product according to their preferences, needs, or tastes. You aim to create a unique and personal experience for each customer, enhancing their satisfaction and engagement. The catch also is that after investing time and energy after personalisation and customisation, your clients will be resistant to jump to another provider.

Zazzle is an online platform that specialises in custom printing services for a diverse array of products, including business cards, marketing materials, and promotional items. With Zazzle's intuitive design tools, customers can effortlessly create bespoke designs that reflect their unique branding or personal style, ensuring their printed materials stand out. The platform's extensive range of customisation options allows for unparalleled personalisation, making each item distinctly yours

Affordability

A startup might offer a product or service that focuses on affordability, by providing customers with cost-effective solutions without compromising on quality or performance. These startups aim to cater to a wider audience by offering budget-friendly options, making their products or services more accessible to customers with varying financial situations.

Dollar Shave Club is a subscription-based service that delivers high-quality razors and grooming products to customers at an affordable price. It cuts out the middleman and by selling directly to consumers, the company can offer better products at lower prices, making personal grooming more budget friendly.

Personalisation

A startup might offer a product or service that focuses on personalisation, by tailoring their offerings to the unique needs, preferences, or characteristics of individual customers. Personalisation can enhance customer satisfaction and create a stronger connection between the customer and the brand, as it demonstrates the company's commitment to understanding and catering to the specific needs of their clientele.

Stitch Fix is an online styling service that provides personalised clothing and accessory recommendations based on customers' individual style preferences, sizes, and budget. By utilising a combination of data-driven algorithms and human stylists, Stitch Fix curates unique clothing selections for each customer, creating a more tailored and enjoyable shopping experience.

Efficacy

A startup might offer a product or service that focuses on efficacy. It demonstrates that the company's products or services can achieve the desired outcomes, thereby building trust and credibility with their customers.

Grammarly is a writing assistant tool that helps users improve their writing by identifying and correcting grammar, spelling, punctuation, and style errors. With its advanced algorithms and easy-to-use interface, Grammarly has become a popular choice for individuals and businesses seeking an effective solution to enhance the quality of their written communication.

Asana is a project management and team collaboration tool that enables teams to efficiently organise, track, and manage their work. As a streamlined platform for planning and executing tasks, Asana helps businesses increase their productivity and achieve their goals more effectively. Asana is a popular choice for organisations of all sizes looking to optimise their workflow.

Quality

A startup might offer a product or service that focuses on quality, by delivering high-performance, reliable, and durable products that meet or exceed customer expectations. Emphasising quality can help a company differentiate itself from competitors and build a strong reputation for delivering exceptional value to its customers.

Apple is known for its commitment to quality in the design and manufacturing of its electronic devices, such as iPhones, iPads, and Mac computers. By focusing on quality materials, innovative design, and user experience, Apple has built a loyal customer base and a reputation for delivering products that are reliable, long-lasting, and perform at a high level. Interestingly even the packaging of the product is awe inspiring.

Flexibility

A startup might offer a product or service that emphasises flexibility, the solutions that can adapt to the diverse needs of its customers. By offering flexible options, a startup can cater to a wider audience and accommodate the changing preferences or requirements of its users over time.

Slack is a communication and collaboration platform that provides businesses with the flexibility to create custom channels, integrate various applications, and adjust notification settings according to their unique needs. This adaptability has made Slack a popular choice for teams seeking a solution that can evolve with their changing communication requirements. But as the old adage goes: "you can be something for everyone, but not everything for everyone".

Shopify is an e-commerce platform that enables businesses to create and manage their online stores. Offering a wide range of customisable templates, payment options, and third-party integrations, Shopify provides a flexible solution for businesses of all sizes to build and scale their e-commerce operations while tailoring the solution according to specific needs and preferences.

Convenience Benefits

These are the benefits that a product or service provides in terms of saving time, effort, or resources. For example, a customer may be willing to pay for online grocery delivery because it saves them the time and effort of going to the store, or for a subscription service because it provides convenient access to a range of products or services. As I have mentioned prior, people are lazy, busy or want things easy. Here are some of the benefits that help with those aspects.

Timesaving

A startup might develop a product or service focused on timesaving, allowing customers to accomplish tasks more efficiently and free up valuable time. By streamlining processes and eliminating unnecessary steps, these startups empower users to allocate their time more effectively. Time-saving solutions are particularly valuable in today's fast-paced world, where time is a precious commodity.

Evernote is a notetaking and organisation app that streamlines the process of capturing, organising, and finding information. By consolidating notes and files in one place, users can quickly access the information they need, saving time spent searching for documents or ideas.

Accessibility

A startup might offer a product or service that is easily accessible, by being available online or through a mobile app. A startup that provides a mobile app for booking and paying for car rentals might make it easy for customers to access the service from anywhere, at any time.

Portability

A startup might focus on creating products or services that offer portability, enabling customers to use their solutions anywhere and at any time. By prioritising portability, startups can cater to the increasing demand for flexible and on-the-go solutions in our modern, mobile world.

Pocket is an app that allows users to save articles, videos, and other content from the web for offline viewing. This feature makes it possible for users to access their saved content on-the-go, even when an internet connection is not available.

Ease of Use

In our fast-paced tech world, where complexity often overwhelms, the ease of use changes the game and empowers the end user. It's a critical factor in product adoption and customer satisfaction. Simplified and intuitive products don't just attract users; they turn them into advocates. Let's explore how two industry giants, Dropbox and Canva, revolutionised user experience.

In a digital age where data is king, managing a myriad of files across multiple devices can be daunting. It all started with a simple yet universal problem: managing numerous files across multiple devices. Dropbox addressed this by creating a user-friendly platform that made file sharing and storage accessible to everyone, regardless of their tech savvy. Dropbox stands out with its user-friendly cloud storage service. It simplifies file management by offering a straightforward interface that caters to all levels of technical expertise. Users can effortlessly store, access, and share files across various devices, eliminating the complexities typically associated with digital storage. This ease of access translates to significant time savings and reduced frustration for users, enhancing productivity and promoting a stress-free digital environment.

Professional graphic design has long been the domain of experts, leaving those without specialised skills feeling overwhelmed. Canva began with a mission to make design easy for everyone. It transformed the complex process of graphic designing into a user-friendly experience, empowering users with no prior design background to create stunning visuals. Canva breaks these barriers by offering a graphic design platform that is intuitive and accessible. Its drag-and-drop interface, coupled with a comprehensive library of templates and design elements, empowers users to create sophisticated designs without prior design experience. Canva simplifies the design process and instils confidence in users, enabling them to unleash their creativity and produce professional-quality designs.

How can your startup simplify its offerings to enhance the user experience? Consider the obstacles your target audience faces and how you can alleviate them with straightforward solutions.

Embracing simplicity in technology goes beyond just removing complexities; it's about enhancing user empowerment and opening new avenues of innovation. This approach aligns with the 'KISS' principle: (Keep It Simple, Stupid), which advocates for simplicity in design and function to improve performance and user experience. As you craft your product or service, prioritise the user's journey, ensuring that every feature adds value and ease.

For a deeper understanding, consider exploring 'Don't Make Me Think' by Steve Krug, a seminal book that delves into the importance of intuitive navigation and user-friendly design in technology. This book can serve as a valuable resource, offering insights into creating products that are functional and a delight to use.

One-stop Shopping

'One Stop Shop' approach is redefining customer convenience. This model, centralising diverse offerings in one platform, is key to attracting and retaining customers. Let's examine how two Australian startups have successfully implemented this strategy.

Busy lifestyles often prevent individuals from planning and preparing healthy meals. HelloFresh Australia offers a one-stop solution for meal planning and preparation. Their service provides pre-portioned ingredients and easy-to-follow recipes delivered directly to homes, simplifying the cooking process. This streamlined approach saves time and reduces the stress of meal planning, leading to a healthier lifestyle for their customers.

Consumers are increasingly looking for eco-friendly shopping options but often must visit multiple stores to find such products. Flora & Fauna is an Australian startup that offers an array of eco-friendly products, from beauty items to home goods, all in one online platform. Their focus is on providing sustainable and ethical options for conscious consumers. By consolidating a wide range of eco-friendly products, Flora & Fauna makes sustainable shopping more accessible and convenient, appealing to environmentally conscious consumers.

Think about how your startup can combine multiple services or products to offer a comprehensive solution. What pain points do your potential customers have, and how can you address them under one umbrella?

Simplicity

Simplicity goes beyond design principle; it's a strategic imperative. This approach, focusing on straightforward and easy-to-use solutions, significantly enhances user engagement and satisfaction. Let's examine how two Australian startups have harnessed simplicity to great effect.

The traditional credit and loan systems can be complex and intimidating for many consumers. Afterpay revolutionised the retail sector with its simple yet effective buy now, pay later service. This straightforward approach allows consumers to make purchases without the immediate financial burden, splitting payments into manageable installments. Afterpay's simplicity has made it popular among consumers, offering a transparent and user-friendly alternative to traditional credit.

Finding reliable help for tasks and small jobs can often be a cumbersome process. Airtasker simplifies this by offering a platform where users can easily connect with local service providers for a wide range of tasks, from home repairs to event planning. By providing a simple, efficient way to hire help, Airtasker has become a go-to solution for Australians needing assistance with everyday tasks. Think about how your startup can reduce complexity in its offerings. Simplicity in design, process, or user experience can set your business apart in a crowded market.

Speed

Speed is a critical factor for growth and competitiveness. Rapid development, quick decision-making, and swift market entry can significantly impact a startup's success. Let's explore how two Australian startups have leveraged speed to gain a competitive edge.

In the tech industry, staying ahead of rapidly evolving trends and technologies is a constant challenge. Atlassian has excelled by rapidly developing and deploying software solutions that meet the changing needs of businesses. Their ability to quickly adapt and innovate has been crucial in their rise to become a global leader in collaboration tools. The speed at which Atlassian delivers updates and new features ensures that their customers always have access to the latest and most efficient tools.

In the financial sector, traditional processes can often be slow and cumbersome. Zip Co offers fast and accessible financial services, including quick approval for payment plans. Their streamlined processes significantly reduce the waiting time for customers. Zip Co's emphasis on speed enhances the customer experience by providing immediate financial solutions, making it an attractive option for those seeking quick and easy financial services.

Assess how your startup can improve its speed in product development, customer service, or market entry. Speed can be a major differentiator in a crowded market.

Convenient Locations

The strategic choice of location can significantly impact a startup's growth and visibility. Here's how two United States-based startups used their locations to enhance their business success.

For consumer-facing businesses like cafes, foot traffic and ambiance are key. Blue Bottle Coffee smartly chose locations in high-foot-traffic areas and urban centres, making their cafes easily accessible and inviting. These prime locations helped Blue Bottle not only attract a consistent flow of customers, but also enhance their brand as a premium coffee experience.

In retail, particularly for fashion and lifestyle brands, physical presence and accessibility are crucial. 'The Warby Parker Solution' by Warby Parker: strategically placed its stores in trendy neighbourhoods and bustling urban centers, ensuring visibility and ease of access. These locations have effectively drawn in customers, reinforcing Warby Parker's image as a trendy and accessible eyewear brand.

Think about how your startup's location can support your business objectives. Whether it's for attracting customers, creating brand identity, or accessing specific markets, the right location can be a significant asset. How can you harness foot traffic data or vehicle traffic data that can give your brand an extended exposure.

High Availability

24/7 availability can be a game-changer for startups, offering a significant competitive advantage. This approach caters to the increasing consumer expectation for round-the-clock access to services and products. Let's explore how two U.S.-based startups have capitalised on this concept.

In e-commerce, customer service expectations are high, with demand for support at all hours. Zappos, an online shoe and clothing retailer, offers 24/7 customer service, ensuring that customers can receive assistance at any time, enhancing the overall shopping experience. This commitment to constant availability has earned Zappos a reputation for exceptional customer service, fostering customer loyalty and trust.

The need for reliable transportation doesn't adhere to a 9-to-5 schedule. Lyft, a ride-sharing service, operates 24/7, providing customers with transportation options at any hour, which is especially critical in urban areas and for late-night services. Lyft's around-the-clock availability has made it a preferred choice for many users who need flexible and reliable transportation options.

Consider how your startup can offer services or support 24/7. This might involve online resources, customer service, or product accessibility.

Adaptability

Adaptability in products or services is crucial for startups to meet diverse customer needs. By offering versatile solutions, startups can enhance customer convenience and widen their market appeal. Let's examine how two U.S. startups have embraced this principle.

In urban living spaces, where square footage is at a premium, versatile furniture solutions are in high demand. Ori, specialising in robotic furniture, offers products that are highly adaptable. Their modular designs can easily transform to fit different room layouts, maximising space utility. Ori's innovative furniture provides a multifunctional, space-saving solution, appealing to customers in compact living environments.

Keeping track of personal items is a common issue for many. Tile offers small, attachable Bluetooth trackers that can be used on a variety of items, from keys to wallets, making them easily locatable. The adaptability of Tile trackers to different objects offers a convenient solution to a universal problem, enhancing daily convenience for users. It has also helped many track the lost luggage which was stranded at an airport thousands of miles away.

Consider how your product or service can be adaptable to different user needs or environments. This flexibility can be a major draw for a diverse customer base.

Health Benefits

These are the benefits that a product or service provides in terms of improving or maintaining physical or mental health. For example, a customer may be willing to pay for a gym membership or personal training sessions because it helps them to stay fit and healthy, or for a meditation app because it helps them to manage stress and improve their mental well-being.

Dental Insurance

Dental insurance is a proactive approach to maintaining oral health, extending beyond mere cost coverage. This section underscores how companies can significantly benefit their employees and customers through comprehensive dental care coverage.

Delta Dental's plans focus on routine cleanings and preventative care, ensuring regular access to crucial dental services. This proactive approach helps avert more severe dental issues, contributing to overall oral wellness. Evaluate how incorporating a dental insurance plan into your benefits package could enhance the long-term oral health of both employees and customers. Does your plan encourage preventative care and include essential treatments? Reflect on how such a plan can elevate overall wellness and satisfaction.

Incorporating a range of dental procedures into insurance plans can substantially impact the wellbeing and financial security of your employees and customers.

Cigna's dental plans cover a wide array of procedures, from routine care to significant treatments like fillings and extractions. This comprehensive coverage relieves financial stress associated with unexpected dental expenses.

Consider the breadth of your dental coverage. How does it alleviate concerns about major dental procedures? Assess the peace of mind it provides, ensuring your employees and customers feel secure against costly dental issues.

Effectively communicating the advantages of dental insurance is vital. It's essential that both your employees and customers understand that this benefit is more than a financial safety net; it's a commitment to their overall health and wellbeing. Your communication should highlight the all-encompassing nature of dental coverage, stressing its contribution to overall health, beyond just financial security.

Body Parts Insurance

Specialised body part insurance goes beyond the traditional notion of risk mitigation. This type of insurance, whether it's for vision, legs, tongue, or any other specific body part, represents a much broader concept. This section elucidates how such insurance policies offer profound benefits at a higher abstraction level, focusing on emotional and practical advantages rather than just the physical aspects of coverage.

Football star Cristiano Ronaldo reportedly insured his legs for a significant amount, reflecting not just the physical value but the peace of mind it provides. This allows him to focus on his sport without the fear of a career-ending injury. In 2009, Real Madrid made headlines by insuring Cristiano Ronaldo's legs for a staggering $144 million (Reference: "Cristiano Ronaldo's Leg Insurance," Forbes Magazine).

Reflect on how your insurance offerings transcend physical protection. Are they structured to alleviate fears and provide mental ease to your clients? How do they enable your clients to pursue their passions or careers unencumbered by worry?

Famed chef Gordon Ramsay insured his tongue for millions, understanding that his taste is essential to his culinary success. This coverage is crucial for the stability of his numerous restaurant businesses (Reference: "Gordon Ramsay's Tongue Insurance," Bloomberg Businessweek). How does your insurance plan contribute to the ongoing success and stability of your clients' professional lives? Does it offer solutions that go beyond individual protection and extend into safeguarding their livelihood?

Notable eye surgeon Dr. Patricia Bath took out insurance on her eyes, recognising the critical role her vision plays in her profession and the importance of a safety net for her surgical practice ("Dr. Patricia Bath's Vision Insurance," The Lancet).

Consider how your insurance policies empower your clients. Do they provide a sense of freedom to operate at their best, knowing they have a safety net in place? How do they mitigate risks in a way that enhances personal and professional confidence? Your communication strategy should emphasise the abstract benefits of these insurance policies.

Rather than focusing on the fear of loss, highlight how these policies empower and protect the clients' lifestyles, careers, and passions.

Retirement Benefits

When it comes to employee wellness and financial planning, retirement benefits go well beyond being a financial tool; they represent a commitment to the long-term well-being and security of employees. This segment explores how companies, through comprehensive retirement benefits, can create a profound emotional and financial impact on their workforce.

Known for its employee-focused retirement plans, Vanguard offers robust 401(k) plans with generous matching contributions. This aids in financial planning and instils a sense of security and appreciation among employees.

Do you offer retirement benefits or consider at some stage in your venture? Will your retirement benefits package provide substantial long-term financial security? How does it enhance your employees' sense of stability and appreciation? Would this give them a reason to belong with your business?

Google's retirement benefits extend beyond standard 401(k) plans, including aspects like financial planning services. This holistic approach offers financial security and emotional aspects of planning for the future. This has enabled many employees to retire in their early thirties and explore other aspects of life and the world.

How do your retirement benefits address the emotional aspects of financial planning? Are there additional services or support that could be provided to enhance peace of mind?

Environmental Benefits

These are the benefits that a product or service provides in terms of reducing negative impacts on the environment. For example, a customer may be willing to pay a premium for eco-friendly products because they want to reduce their carbon footprint, or for a car with good fuel efficiency because it reduces their environmental impact. It may not seem obvious at the first instance, but your aim is to embed emotion in your offering.

Green Energy

In today's market, environmental awareness is increasingly significant (though sometimes perceived as a trend by some organisations), initiatives like carbon offsetting in the aviation industry represent more than just eco-responsibility. They serve as a powerful means to forge emotional connections with customers. Airlines, committed to reducing their environmental impact, can deepen their relationship with passengers through sustainable practices.

Qantas has taken a notable step in environmental stewardship with its carbon offset program. By offering passengers the option to pay extra for carbon offsets, Qantas not only works towards neutralising its carbon footprint but also allows customers to be active participants in this initiative.

How can your company integrate similar sustainable practices? Does your business model allow customers to directly contribute to environmental initiatives, enhancing their sense of responsibility and involvement?

Delta's commitment to sustainability goes beyond its own operations. By engaging in community projects and partnerships focused on sustainability, they create a broader, community-centric approach to environmental responsibility. How does your company's sustainability strategy extend to community involvement? Are there ways you can encourage collective action for environmental causes among your customers?

Emirates has implemented various sustainability measures, including reducing single-use plastics on flights. Their efforts towards a more sustainable operation model not only reduce waste but also signify a commitment to future generations.

As a founder, what steps is your company taking towards long-term environmental sustainability? How are these efforts shaping the legacy and future perception of your brand?

Energy Efficiency

In today's eco-conscious market, energy efficiency is a significant driver of business value and customer engagement. This section delves into how businesses adopting energy-efficient practices and products can reap benefits that extend beyond cost savings, fostering customer loyalty and enhancing brand reputation.

Philips has set a benchmark in energy efficiency with its LED lighting solutions. By offering products that significantly reduce energy consumption, Philips not only aids customers in cutting down utility costs but also contributes to a reduction in global carbon emissions.

How can your business incorporate energy-efficient solutions? Consider the impact of such offerings on both your customers' expenses and your company's environmental footprint.

Whirlpool's range of energy-efficient appliances showcases how integrating energy-saving features can enhance customer satisfaction. These products appeal to the growing segment of environmentally aware consumers, strengthening the brand's relationship with its customers.

Tesla's advancements in energy-efficient electric vehicles and solar energy products have transformed the automotive and energy sectors and set new sustainability standards. Tesla's commitment to energy efficiency positions the brand as a visionary leader in the drive towards a sustainable future.

Reflect on how your products can be redesigned for better energy efficiency. How can this shift help in building stronger, value-based relationships with your customers? What role can your business play in setting industry standards for energy efficiency? How can your commitment to energy efficiency elevate your brand's status in the market?

Sustainable Products and Services

Sustainability is increasingly at the forefront of consumer consciousness, the shift towards sustainable products represents a significant opportunity for businesses. This section explores how offering sustainable products goes beyond environmental benefits, forging a powerful emotional connection with customers and positioning businesses as leaders in social responsibility.

Allbirds, a company specialising in sustainable footwear, exemplifies the benefits of aligning product design with environmental consciousness. Their shoes, made from natural and recycled materials, not only minimise ecological impact but also resonate with customers' growing preference for eco-friendly products.

How can your product line be adapted or expanded to include sustainable options? Consider how this shift could align with your customers' values and potentially open new market segments.

Lush Cosmetics' commitment to zero-waste products, like shampoo bars and package-free items, reduces environmental impact and builds deep brand loyalty. Customers feel a part of Lush's sustainability journey, further solidifying their connection to the brand.

Tesla has redefined the automotive industry with its electric vehicles, setting a new standard for sustainable innovation. Beyond reducing carbon emissions, Tesla's products symbolise a commitment to a cleaner, more sustainable future, appealing to consumers' desire to be part of this change.

Reflect on how your business can incorporate zero-waste or minimal packaging strategies. How can these practices strengthen your brand identity and customer loyalty? What long-term impacts can your sustainable products achieve? Consider how innovation in sustainability can position your company as a leader in your industry and capture the imagination of your customers.

Waste Reduction

In the contemporary marketplace, where ecological consciousness is paramount (some organisations on the planet may be just following the fad), waste reduction transcends mere environmental responsibility. It's a conduit for creating emotional resonance with customers. This exploration delves into how businesses, through their commitment to waste reduction, can cultivate a deeper emotional connection with their audience. Number of circular economy businesses have emerged from this idea.

Renowned for its environmental advocacy, Patagonia's initiatives, like the Worn Wear program, encourage customers to repair, share, and recycle their gear. This approach not only reduces waste but also fosters a deep sense of participation in environmental stewardship.

TerraCycle's mission is to eliminate the idea of waste. By partnering with companies to recycle hard-to-recycle materials, they create a community-focused approach to waste reduction, making the consumer an active participant in this mission.

IKEA's sustainability plan, including efforts to become circular and climate positive by 2030, is a commitment to future generations. They offer products designed with recyclable materials and solutions for product life extension.

Are your products designed for longevity and recyclability? How does your brand encourage consumers to participate in waste reduction? How does your service or product create a sense of community around waste reduction? Are there opportunities for customer involvement in your sustainability efforts? How does your company's approach to waste reduction contribute to a sustainable future? What legacy are you building through your environmental initiatives?

Environmental Education

Our current day to day lives are attuned to the importance of sustainability, environmental education stands as a crucial element for businesses, going beyond mere information dissemination. This section illuminates how companies integrating environmental education into their operations can yield profound benefits, not only for the environment but also for their customer relationships and brand perception.

IKEA has integrated environmental education into its customer experience through sustainable living workshops. These sessions empower customers with knowledge about eco-friendly practices and products, facilitating informed and conscious choices.

National Geographic, known for its stunning visual storytelling, combines its media platforms with educational content on environmental issues. This approach informs and inspires a global audience, contributing to a legacy of environmental awareness.

How can your business educate customers about environmental sustainability? Consider ways to incorporate educational elements into your products or services that guide customers toward making environmentally friendly choices. What steps can your company take to integrate environmental education into your content or marketing strategies? How can this foster a deeper understanding and appreciation of sustainability issues among your audience?

Green Building Design

The move towards green building design is more than a trend in architecture and construction; it's a fundamental shift in how businesses approach sustainability. This section explores how the integration of green building practices not only benefits the environment but also enhances the well-being of occupants, leading to a deeper connection with clients and stakeholders.

The Edge in Amsterdam, often hailed as one of the world's greenest buildings, exemplifies the benefits of green design. Utilising natural light, energy-efficient systems, and indoor air quality controls, it creates a workspace that's not just environmentally friendly, but also conducive to employee health and productivity.

Salesforce Tower's green design includes publicly accessible spaces that foster community engagement, alongside its eco-friendly construction. This approach reduces environmental impact and strengthens the bond between the business and the local community.

The Bosco Verticale in Milan, with its vertical forests, is an architectural marvel; it's a statement of environmental responsibility. The building addresses urban air quality and biodiversity, showcasing a profound commitment to ecological concerns.

How can your business's physical spaces reflect a commitment to sustainability? Consider the potential impact of natural lighting, energy-saving measures, and green spaces on employee well-being and productivity. Reflect on how your building or workspace can become a hub for community interaction and environmental education. How can your facilities serve as a model for sustainable practices in your community? What long-term environmental impacts can your building designs achieve? Consider how incorporating elements like green walls or renewable energy sources can set a precedent in your industry.

Quality Benefits

These are the benefits that a product or service provides in terms of superior quality or performance. For example, a customer may be willing to pay for a high-end appliance because it is more reliable and performs better, or for a luxury hotel because it provides a higher level of comfort and service. Quality is often a blend of tangible and intangible. Tangible is around what is being offered and intangible is around how it is offered.

Product or Service Quality

For startups, the quality of products or services often is the core of business success and customer loyalty. This section delves into how startups, through a relentless focus on quality, can carve out a unique space in the market.

Dyson has been a player in a competitive consumer market where innovation and quality were the key drivers. Dyson transformed the home appliance industry with high-quality, innovative designs. Their products, particularly vacuum cleaners, are a testament to excellence in engineering and user-centric design. Dyson's emphasis on quality has earned it a loyal following and set a benchmark in the appliance industry, proving that quality drives both customer satisfaction and brand leadership.

Zoom went through substantial growth over the last few years and has managed to disrupt the market despite having strong incumbents like Microsoft (teams) and many other players who offer solutions in the service industry. in video conferencing. The reason has been that it caters to technical quality and an excellent user experience. I have seen users switch from other platforms to Zoom just because of this one reason. They've become synonymous with dependable and accessible video conferencing. Zoom emerged as a leader by offering high-quality, reliable, and user-friendly video conferencing services. They focused on seamless connectivity and ease of use, crucial for both individual and corporate clients.

Scrutinise how your startup can embody quality in every facet, from initial design to after-sales service. Quality should be the defining trait of your offering.

Customer Service

Exceptional customer service certainly helps in today's market which is becoming more and more competitive. Users want results at lightning speed almost in real time.

Delivering consistent, high-quality customer experiences is vital in the digital age. Cyara offers an automated platform for businesses to test and monitor their customer service systems, ensuring efficiency and quality in customer interactions. By using Cyara, companies can enhance their customer service, leading to improved satisfaction and loyalty.

In the beauty industry, creating a personalised and responsive customer experience is key. Glossier has built its brand by engaging directly with customers, using their feedback to shape product development and offering personalised customer service. This approach has fostered a loyal community, with customers feeling valued and heard.

Consider how your startup can integrate exceptional customer service. From using technology to personal interactions to involving customers in product development, the goal is to create a service culture that resonates with your audience.

For startups, exceptional customer service is often left to support. Often customers reach out when there is a dispute or a problem. Once resolved, it is reflected as pain is now taken away... but scars are there. It should be a strategic tool that drives growth and builds loyalty by providing help and assistance so that the customer is less likely to complain in the first place. Automation tools and AI are now becoming commonplace to do so.

What do you intend to do in your business that can help you in the long run?

Employee Training and Development

For startups, investing in employee training and development is essential for sustaining growth and fostering innovation. Often it is seen as the cost to the business. The question that is often asked - what if they leave after training. The question that should be asked is what if they are trained and they leave. Growing up, I recall TCS or Tata Consulting Services, invested heavily in training programs in the earlier years of all staff including software development. The ceiling was set very high in these programs to be successful. The outcome is that besides expertise the organisation has an awesome working culture and has a lion's share of business in a number of global organisations without relying on heavy advertising.

Keeping employees skilled and innovative is crucial. Google sets a high standard with its comprehensive employee development programs. They offer a variety of training, from technical skills to leadership development, creating an environment of continuous learning and innovation. This commitment to employee growth has helped Google maintain its position as a leader in tech innovation, attracting and retaining top talent.

In the competitive world of CRM and cloud computing, maintaining a knowledgeable and adaptable workforce is key. Salesforce's focus on employee training encompasses a range of programs, emphasising both professional and personal development. Their dedication to empowering employees has been a cornerstone of their success. By investing in their workforce, Salesforce has enhanced its service quality and fostered a culture of loyalty and innovation.

Often you will find that with the proliferation of technologies there are many avenues to do self-study, books (you are reading one), podcasts, YouTube, Udemy, online courses and universities which offer free information have truly reduced the barrier to learning. Time and inclination are going to be the key drivers. I would suggest a three pronged approach to learning:

1. Institutional or from startup: you can offer formal education or training based on their career path.
2. Employees can do at their own pace or online: this may compliment their existing learning or if they want to learn something outside their core work.
3. On the job learning: perhaps by solving real world problems.
4. Shadowing: if someone is successful, try and understand them, understand the actions and the reasoning behind it.

Besides, when the technology grows in leaps and bounds your workforce may start falling behind. Hiring new staff does offer an option, however reskilling the workforce may be a cost effective solution. Besides the benefit of risk management to you as a founder it gives business continuity and creates loyalty among staff that you want to retain.

Assess your startup's approach to training and development. Is there a culture that encourages continual learning? Are there opportunities for employees to grow both professionally and personally?

Continuous Improvement

Even a mature industry like the automotive industry is evolving quickly with new technologies and sustainability demands. Toyota's Kaizen philosophy focuses on efficiency and adaptability. Their continuous improvement practices enable them to stay ahead in an industry undergoing rapid technological and environmental changes. This adaptability has allowed Toyota to remain competitive and innovative, even as the automotive industry faces significant shifts.

In the rapidly advancing field of AI and graphics technology, staying ahead requires relentless innovation. Nvidia's commitment to continuous improvement is evident in their iterative development and aggressive investment in new technologies. By focusing on enhancing performance and expanding their technology's capabilities, Nvidia stays at the cutting edge. Nvidia has emerged as a leader in AI and graphics, consistently pushing the boundaries of what is possible and setting new standards in the industry. The astronomical market capitalisation at the time of writing this segment on 18th June 2024 stands at 3.22 trillion which is far greater than many world economies.

Your startup can draw inspiration from these giants. Consider how continuous improvement can be applied to your business, not just for efficiency, but for adaptability and leadership in your industry. In addition to Kaizen, methodologies like Six Sigma and Lean can be instrumental for startups. Six Sigma focuses on reducing process variation and improving quality, while Lean emphasises waste reduction and streamlining operations. Integrating these methodologies can provide a comprehensive toolkit for startups aiming to optimise processes and maintain competitive agility in their industries.

Customer Loyalty: The Role of Intergenerational Retention

Loyalty in business is a multifaceted concept, encompassing more than just customer retention. It involves creating deep-rooted connections with customers, leading to sustained business success. Loyal customers often translate to repeat business, word-of-mouth promotion, and a reliable revenue stream. They are also more likely to provide valuable feedback and be forgiving of minor mistakes. From a business perspective, cultivating loyalty is cost-effective compared to acquiring new customers. It requires understanding customer needs, consistently delivering quality, and creating emotional connections. Building loyalty is about fostering trust and ensuring customers feel valued and understood.

Products

Loyalty can transcend generations. Intergenerational loyalty in businesses can have exceptional examples like Patek Philippe and Steinway & Sons, and of course, many elite educational institutions represents a bidirectional commitment between the brand and its customers.

Patek Philippe: A Legacy of Trust: Patek Philippe has fostered loyalty by ensuring exceptional quality and timeless value in their watches, appealing to each generation's desire for heritage and prestige. Customers remain loyal due to the brand's commitment to quality and the brand reciprocates by maintaining standards and values that resonate across ages.

Steinway & Sons: Harmonising Quality and Legacy: Standing out in the competitive world of musical instruments. Steinway pianos, known for their unparalleled craftsmanship, create an emotional and musical legacy, cherished by families and institutions. The brand's dedication to quality ensures customer loyalty, and this loyalty, in turn, fuels the brand's commitment to excellence.

Educational Institutions

Many schools or educational institutions in Australia foster a legacy of excellence and community can also exemplify this bidirectional loyalty. They create an enduring educational heritage, which families value across generations. In many cases I have observed that the parents enrol their newborns in their own school on or around the day of their birth (for a definitive entry) to ensure the legacy continues in the family.

Consider how your startup can build a legacy that encourages this kind of deep, enduring loyalty. It's about creating value that transcends generations and nurturing a relationship that grows over time.

Intergenerational loyalty is a mutual, enduring commitment. It's about brands consistently delivering excellence and customers valuing this legacy, creating a cycle of trust and loyalty that spans generations.

| 10 |

Appropriating the Benefit: Setting the Right Price

You have given the benefit to your customer and now it is time to appropriate it. The key determinant for you is what is the price you capture. There are situations and circumstances where your customer is a contributor (content, ideas, marketplaces) that is however beyond the discussion of the current version of the book.

Low Price

This strategy involves offering a product or service at a lower price than competitors to attract price-sensitive customers. This approach undercuts competitors by offering similar quality products at a lower price. Walmart, for example, embraces this strategy, focusing on every-day low prices as a primary selling point. In a business where the competitive intensity is high, and you are working on transactional products you can look into everyday low prices. However, as a startup you are often revamping the business models so it is less likely that you will focus on this type of pricing.

Differentiated

This strategy involves offering a unique product or service that is not easily comparable to competitors' offerings and charging a premium price for it. Businesses justify higher prices due to the distinctive value offered. Apple embodies this strategy, offering high-end, innovative technology that differentiates them from competitors. It is very likely that you may focus on this type of strategy in a startup. I have heard from Kanwal Rekhi, (VC who has been instrumental in the success of large number of startups worldwide and is also a founder of TiE, a non-profit organisation that supports entrepreneurs through mentoring, networking, education, funding, and incubation) believes that raising prices can signal value and quality, thereby attracting more serious customers and investors, ultimately boosting the company's market position and profitability. Exodus Communications, Poshmark, Excelan, CyberMedia are few noteworthy examples.

Cost-plus Pricing

This strategy involves setting the price of a product or service by adding a markup to the cost of production. This straightforward pricing approach is frequently used in retail, like in independent bookstores, where the retail price often is the wholesale cost plus a standard markup.

Penetration Pricing

This strategy involves setting a low (or no) initial price for a product or service to quickly gain market share, with the intention of raising prices once the product or service has gained popularity. Businesses set a low initial price to lure customers, intending to raise the price later. Amazon used this strategy with Kindle, pricing it low initially to boost its adoption. As a startup founder this is the area where you will spend most of your time building your understanding.

Tactics for Price Increases

As the customer base grows, the startup gradually increases prices or introduces paid features. This approach can involve several tactics:

Free Initial Offering: startups may offer their core product or service for free to attract early users. This is common in software and app-based companies. For instance, companies like Dropbox and Slack initially offer free versions with limited features.

Freemium Model: the startup provides a basic version of the product for free while offering premium features or services at a cost. This allows users to experience the product without financial commitment and can drive conversion to paid plans. Examples include Spotify and LinkedIn.

Feature Additions: as the product matures and more features are added, the startup can introduce tiered pricing. Basic features remain free, but advanced functionalities are offered at different price points. This helps in monetising while still retaining a large user base.

Grandfathering: early adopters who start using the product for free are often 'grandfathered' into their free plans even after the company introduces paid versions. This rewards loyalty and helps maintain goodwill among early users. Evernote has used this approach effectively.

Gradual Price Increase: over time, as the value of the product is proven and users become dependent on it, prices are gradually increased. Users who are already engaged are more likely to continue using the service even at a higher price. This was seen with Netflix as it transitioned from a low-cost DVD rental service to a leading streaming service with higher subscription fees.

Dropbox started with free storage to attract users and then introduced paid plans with more storage and features. Slack was initially free for small teams with limited features, then offered paid plans for larger teams and additional functionalities. Spotify used a free tier with ads and limitations, premium tier without ads and additional features. Penetration pricing helps startups quickly build a user base, gather feedback, and create a strong market presence. However, the challenge lies in effectively transitioning users from free to paid plans without losing their loyalty. You may need to work on strategies on effective transition which are beyond the scope of this book.

Economy Pricing

This strategy involves offering a basic product or service at a low price to appeal to budget-conscious customers. An example of this would be budget airlines like Jetstar, which offer no-frills flight services at the lowest possible prices.

Price Skimming

This strategy involves setting a high initial price for a product or service, then gradually lowering the price over time as competitors enter the market and demand for the product or service decreases. This strategy is common with new technology, such as the PlayStation console releases, starting high and then gradually lowering the price. Skimming pricing leverages "Crossing the Chasm"[4] principles by targeting early adopters who are willing to pay a premium for the latest innovations. These early adopters, often called 'tech enthusiasts' or 'visionaries', queue up to be the first to own new products because they value cutting-edge technology and the prestige of being early owners. This strategy helps startups quickly recoup development costs while building market presence before lowering prices to attract a broader, more price-sensitive customer base.

Premium Pricing

This strategy involves setting a high price for a product or service to convey its quality, exclusivity, or luxury status. This often works for brands that offer high-quality products or services, like Rolex watches, projecting an image of luxury, exclusivity, and superior craftsmanship. Just charging high prices in the pretence of high quality may not be sustainable as disillusionment from the promise may deteriorate brand value rapidly.

Psychological Pricing

This strategy involves setting prices that have a psychological effect on customers, such as using odd numbers or prices that end in '9' to make the product or service seem more attractive. For example, 9.99 or 9.95 feels better than 10.00. It's a subtle perception game but proves quite effective.

Notes

1. A TED talk by Bill Gross The Single Biggest Reason Why Start-ups Succeed, discusses market timing as the largest factor of success of a venture

2. The Strategy Canvas - Blue Ocean Strategy by Kim and Mauborgne

3. Sangeet Paul Choudhary's two books are -
   Platform Scale for a Post-Pandemic World

   Platform Revolution: How Networked Markets Are Transforming the Economy and How to Make Them Work for You: How Networked Markets Are Transforming the Economy—and How to Make Them Work for You

4. Crossing the Chasm, Marketing and Selling Disruptive Products to Mainstream Customers Paperback – by Geoffrey A Moore

Continue Your Journey

1. **Ries, Eric.** *The Lean Startup.* Crown Business, 2011.
   - Focuses on building agile and adaptable startups with customer feedback and iterative development.
2. **Blank, Steve, and Bob Dorf.** *The Startup Owner's Manual: The Step-By-Step Guide for Building a Great Company.* K&S Ranch, 2012.
   - Comprehensive guidelines on starting a business with an emphasis on customer discovery and validation.
3. **Kawasaki, Guy.** *The Art of Start 2.0: The Time-Tested, Battle-Hardened Guide for Anyone Starting Anything.* John Wiley & Sons, 2010.
   - Practical advice on turning ideas into successful ventures.
4. **Christensen, Clayton M.** *The Innovator's Dilemma: When New Technologies Cause Great Firms to Fail.* Harvard Business Review Press, 1997.
   - Discusses how companies can fail even when doing everything right and highlights the importance of innovation.
5. **Cooper, Brant, and Patrick Vlaskovits.** *The Lean Entrepreneur: How Constant Innovation Creates Radically Successful Businesses.* John Wiley & Sons, 2013.
   - Explains the role of continuous innovation in building a successful business.
6. **Olsen, Dan.** *The Lean Product Playbook: How to Innovate with Minimum Viable Products and Rapid Customer Feedback.* John Wiley & Sons, 2015.
   - A guide to developing products that customers love using lean principles.
7. **Wasserman, Noam.** *The Founder's Dilemmas: Anticipating and Avoiding the Pitfalls That Can Sink a Startup.* Princeton University Press, 2012.
   - Addresses common challenges faced by entrepreneurs.
8. **Heath, Chip, and Dan Heath.** *The Power of Moments: Why Certain Experiences Have Extraordinary Impact.* Simon & Schuster, 2017.
   - Explores the impact of defining moments in business and life.
9. **Hsieh, Tony.** *Delivering Happiness: A Path to Profits, Passion, and Purpose.* Business Plus, 2010.

- Insights on building a strong company culture and delivering customer experiences.

10. **Fitzpatrick, Rob.** *The Mom Test: How to talk to customers & learn if your business is a good idea when everyone is lying to you.* Createspace Independent Publishing Platform, 2013.
    - Practical advice on effectively talking to customers and validating business ideas.

11. **Pine, B. Joseph, and James H. Gilmore.** *The Experience Economy.* Harvard Business Review Press, 1999.
    - Discusses the shift towards experiences as primary economic offerings.

12. **Osterwalder, Alexander, et al.** *Value Proposition Design: How to Create Products and Services Customers Want.* John Wiley & Sons, 2014.
    - A guide to creating products and services that meet customer desires.

13. **Maurya, Ash.** *Running Lean: Iterate from Plan A to a Plan That Works.* O'Reilly Media, 2012.
    - A process for iterating from plan A to a successful plan in startup creation.

14. **Kim, W. Chan, and Renée Mauborgne.** *Blue Ocean Strategy: How to Create Uncontested Market Space and Make the Competition Irrelevant.* Harvard Business Review Press, 2005.
    - A seminal book on creating new market spaces.

15. **Thiel, Peter.** *Zero to One: Notes on Startups, or How to Build the Future.* Crown Business, 2014.
    - Peter Thiel's insights on innovative thinking and unique strategies in startups.

16. **Diamandis, Peter H., and Steven Kotler.** *Bold: How to Go Big, Create Wealth and Impact the World.* Simon & Schuster, 2015.
    - Explores the use of technology and bold thinking in creating significant impacts and innovations.

Sameer Babbar

Entrepreneurship and Innovation evangelist

In the world of startups, Sameer Babbar stands out as a seasoned guide, a technology enthusiast, and a master of business strategy. With roots in engineering and an MBA, Sameer has sculpted a career marked by innovation, risk management, and transformative leadership. He advises on strategy and growth; he breathes life into startup visions, turning bold ideas into market realities.

Sameer's journey transcends typical consulting. He is an equity holder in many startups, a testament to his belief in the potential of groundbreaking ideas. His innovation and entrepreneurship advisor role at SRM University AP, India, and his charter membership at TiE Global highlight his commitment.

His unique approach to entrepreneurship sets Sameer apart: he teaches the art of selling benefits, not just features, to aspiring entrepreneurs. He believes that the essence of a successful venture lies in its ability to solve real-world problems, extending beyond the technical prowess of its offerings. This philosophy is the bedrock of his mentorship and speaking engagements, where he inspires and equips startup founders to craft compelling narratives around their innovations.

In this book, Sameer shares his wisdom on the importance of learning how to articulate the value of your ideas in a way that resonates with customers and investors alike.

Welcome to a journey of discovery, strategy, and success.

www.ingramcontent.com/pod-product-compliance
Lightning Source LLC
Chambersburg PA
CBHW071427210326
41597CB00020B/3690